I SAW THE FUTURE

To Caroline
enjoy the read.
Sophie x

Copyright © 2020 S Jones
All rights reserved.
ISBN: 9798639325106

The cover features a picture of the author's eye. The other eye is brown. The authors true identify is therefore verified by their right eye matching the eye on the cover.

I SAW THE FUTURE

S JONES

Experiences after reading this book:

"After reading this book I had a dream of a sign representing death. The following day my best friend's son died. I believe the symbol was a warning that someone close to me was going to die." - *Cheryl S.*

"I had the profound feeling that I had met a certain person before after reading these stories and realized that I haven't lived my current age before. A knowing activated inside me that I have never been 60 years old before in a past life." - *Barbara Smith*

"Before I read this book, I was an A class skeptic, my partner made me watch some of the documentaries mentioned in the book with her and now I must admit I actually do believe in the paranormal and afterlife. A whole new world has opened up. Seeing people in the documentaries with high qualifications and scientific background coming forward discussing UFOs and actual EMT and frontline workers discuss their paranormal experiences I am starting to open up. My partner started then discussing the dreams from this book and then I actually started dreaming myself which I never noticed before!" -*Andrew N.*

"My intuition has increased I had a thought to buy a specific catering business and were beaten to it. I went and had a burger from it. Two men were serving, and I said to the older one how's business he said, "We've only been here a week and it's a bit slow yet.". People had seen this van not operating for quite some time. There is also competition around the vicinity. I said to the man, "If you can manage not relying on profit for 6 weeks things will go well.". The virus kicked in and I was going that way so stopped for a chat he said, "I'm working until 10pm and am rushed off my feet, how did you know as it's been just over 6 weeks since you said that this would happen and I have been busier than ever since!", I just knew." - *John*

Other books by this author:

How to remember your dreams:
A dream journal workbook to learn to recall, record
and chart your dreams
ISBN-13: 978-1730811401

Table of Contents

INTRODUCTION 13
1. MY BACKGROUND 22
2. THE TRAUMA OF MY FIRST OBE 23
3. THE NIGHTLY SPIN OF THE OBE 25
4. ACTING OUT PAST-LIFE MEMORIES AT NIGHT . 27
5. AS ABOVE SO BELOW 29
6. THE UFO 31
7. THE SPONTANEOUS OBE 34
8. FATHER'S NEAR-DEATH EXPERIENCES 36
9. DISCOVERING DREAMS 38
10. THE PSYCHIC WORKSHOP 41
11. THE SCHOOL TEACHER 43
12. ET CONTACT 44
13. THE OLD MARBLE PILLAR 46
14. A HISTORY ON SIGMUND FREUD 48
15. YOU CAN DIE IN A DREAM 50
16. BEAUTIFUL ASTRAL REALM HOUSE 52
17. TELEPATHIC DREAM CLASSES 54
18. COMETS HIT THE EARTH 56
19. A TELEPATHIC REPTILIAN ENEMY 57
20. THE MYTHICAL AREA 59
21. DRUNKEN ASTRAL REALM ENCOUNTERS 60
22. CURIOSITY INTO LEVITATION 62
23. THE WITCH 65
24. SURVIVAL INSTINCT 66
25. THE SUPERCONSCIOUSNESS 68
26. THE BEAUTIFUL IRIS 73
27. LEVITATION IN FORCE IN THE ASTRAL REALM . 75
28. THE DEMON FIGHT 77
29. A BEAUTIFUL HOUSE 79
30. SECRET ROOM TO ANOTHER WORLD 80
31. FIGHTING IN THE ASTRAL REALM 82
32. THE AFTERLIFE FERRY 83
33. FEELING DRUNK IN THE ASTRAL REALM 85
34. MEETING GREAT GRANDMOTHER 86
35. THE BUDDHA EVENT 88
36. THE BEAUTIFUL CELESITE CRYSTAL DRAWING 89
37. TRAINING ASTRAL PROJECTION/MEDITATION . 90
38. BEAUTIFUL PEACOCK 91
39. THE ASTRAL REALM TOURIST ATTRACTION 92
40. ESP OF OTHERS' INTENTIONS 93
41. THE DESERT BOOKSHOP 94
42. OBE WHILST MEDITATING 95

43.	Entering Someone's Dream	96
44.	Re-entering a Dream	98
45.	Dream Within a Dream	100
46.	Robot Wars	102
47.	Meeting My Subconscious	103
48.	Predictive Dream	104
49.	Predictive Dream: Random Birthday	105
50.	Headache Tablets	106
51.	Internal Thoughts	107
52.	Watching My Friend in Their Dream	108
53.	Same Dream, Difference Perspectives	109
54.	Morphing into a Bat	110
55.	Becoming Lucid in a Dream	112
56.	The Beauty of the Dream World	114
57.	The Food Drama	115
58.	The Time Machine	116
59.	The Buddhist Book	117
60.	Men in Black (MIB)	118
61.	The Superconsciousness Task	120
62.	DNA Structure	121
63.	Soul Group Discussion	122
64.	Through a Tunnel Whilst Mediating	123
65.	The Negative Entity	124
66.	The Beauty of the Trees	125
67.	Guiding an OBE	127
68.	The Intelligent Man	129
69.	The Teachings	130
70.	Continuum of Time & Sleep Paralysis	131
71.	The Evil Lady	134
72.	Seeing a Demon In Another's Dream	135
73.	Reading a Book in the Astral Realm	138
74.	Astral Realm Running	139
75.	Dream Telepathy	140
76.	ESP Dream	141
77.	Going into the Future	142
78.	Blanking Out Dreams	144
79.	OBE After Waking From a Dream	145
80.	Learning to be psychic in a dream	147
81.	Different Perspectives: Shared Dream	148
82.	Blue Alien Amphibious Beings	149
83.	Being a Spiritual Teacher	151
84.	Taught How to be Psychic	152
85.	My Male Anima	153
86.	Nuclear Bomb	154
87.	Conscious Astral Projection At Will	155
88.	The Voice	157

89.	Enjoying the Scene of the Astral Realm	158
90.	The Huge Lucid Dream Mansion	159
91.	The Sharman Necklace	161
92.	Start of an OBE	162
93.	An Amazing Crystal House	163
94.	Bi Location	164
95.	The Incredible Mind of the Future	166
96.	A Future Time Traveler	169
97.	The Prayer Beads	170
98.	A Shape Shifter	171
99.	The Hypnagogic State	172
100.	Thought Form to Create Objects	173
101.	The Trickster Encounter	174
102.	The Egyptian Amulet	176
103.	Discussing a Curse: Elixir	178
104.	Viewing a Friends Dream	179
105.	The Squatters a Shared Dream	180
106.	The Doppelgangers	182
107.	Other Lives	183
108.	The Farmer's Kid	184
109.	Special Forces	185
110.	The Smart Female	188
111.	The Military Camp	189
112.	Fluency in Another Language	191
113.	40 Years as a Male	193
114.	A Man in the Medieval Days	194
115.	The Love Story	195
116.	My Smart Daughter	196
117.	Past Life Regression	197
118.	A Pause in My Dreams	200
119.	Final Thoughts	212

ABOUT THE AUTHOR **214**

List of Illustrations

Illustration 1 Spinning Around 25
Illustration 2 Acting Out a Past-life.................... 27
Illustration 3 The UFO 32
Illustration 4 The Bench 42
Illustration 5 ET Contact 45
Illustration 6 Reptilian eyed man...................... 58
Illustration 7 Levitation Interest 64
Illustration 8 Levitation in Force 75
Illustration 9 The Beautiful Peacock 91
Illustration 10 The Gatekeeper 128
Illustration 11 Demon from a Friends Dream 136
Illustration 12 The Future City 143
Illustration 13 The Angel 155
Illustration 14 The Lucid Dream 160
Illustration 15 Bi Location Planet.................... 165
Illustration 16 I Saw the Future 167
Illustration 17 Egyptian Amulet 176
Illustration 18 Special Services Mission 187
Illustration 19 The Room 192
Illustration 20 Medieval past-life..................... 194
Illustration 21 Baphomet 201
Illustration 22 Trust Your Subconscious 203
Illustration 23 The Peacock Egg...................... 205
Illustration 24 See The Truth 206

PREFACE

One night I saw something that changed my life. I was meditating when I suddenly found myself walking down a corridor, in a spaceship, with an enhanced mind. The level of intelligence I witnessed was incredible and after this experience I became highly focused on recording my experiences and dreams.

I started to ask others if they had experienced similar events and sought out other people that had. I wanted to be able to discuss these unexplained experiences with others and hear about their experiences.

I SAW THE FUTURE, shares a snapshot of all my interesting dreams, meditation experiences, and out of body experiences that I recorded over a two-year period, initially setting the scene with early experiences.

This book aims to inspire you to seek to investigate your own dreams. Likewise, for those who have had similar experiences, the book acts to validate experiences that may have been brushed aside or left the experiencer confused.

Please write to me if you encounter any differences in your dreams after reading this book or have had similar experiences (see contact details at the end).

S Jones
The author

Introduction

Imagine experiencing flying through the universe, feeling at peace, and understanding everything all at once. An intense infinite knowledge of all but at the same time nothing, no pain and pure enjoyment, you do not want it to end. You are aware of everything but at the same time nothing. Hold that feeling. Then imagine coming back to where you are now and having the everyday stresses of the world back on your shoulders.

Now close your eyes and imagine you are suddenly walking down a corridor. You do not know where you are, but you feel it is somewhere in interstellar space. You think of the Earth and suddenly in an instant you are aware of the whole history of humanity and Earth's development. In shock from this sudden knowledge you look at the corridor you are walking down, and you intuitively know all the mathematical equations used to construct this vehicle you are in, this interstellar spaceship. Your brain is incredible, the knowledge at which you comprehend everything is incredible. You come back to the real world and you feel primitive in comparison and wonder if that is how it feels to be a 'genius'.

I wrote this book because I had the above experience and this experience changed my life and opened me up to the beauty of the unknown.

The world of dreaming is powerful, yet few rarely take the time to consider it, ignoring the endless possibilities that lie ahead for them. The endless entertainment, unlimited knowledge, and mysteries of the universe. We often seek ways to be entertained or ways to expand our mind but lack looking inwards for that of which we seek.

Nicola Tesla reported using his dreams to undertake experiments before carrying them out in the physical world. Tesla credited the superconsciousness as the source of his creativity. This superconsciousness is what I talk about in my opening paragraph. Infinite knowledge of everything.

Dreams have been known to be credited to some of the greatest inventions, Nobel prizes and movies. Yet why is it we lack to investigate this potential unlimited source of creatively and entertainment. Why do we not use this unlimited source to solve our problems in life?

People will become alcoholics and drug addicts to achieve entertainment in their lives, destroying their bodies at the same time without knowing they can achieve this high just through their dreams. Which they do every night, unaware of the potential entertainment they are not conscious of and the potential high feelings that they can encounter. No drug can come close to achieving the state of being in the superconsciousness.

Within a period of two years I counted over 600 dreams and dreamt more entertaining dreams than I have watched movies in a lifetime.

My dreams have given me experiences I cannot relay to people, especially the experiences where I cannot describe the feelings I had, as there are no words possible to describe them. Yet at the same time, I have witnessed events in my dreams, that allow me to empathize with others that I would never be able to do in the real world, for example, being a father.

I had a single dream one night, that went on for 40 years, where I was a male, an accountant. I lived his whole life, his nine to five job, waiting for the clock to strike 5pm. The marriage to his wife, the birth of his children, and right up until the day of his daughters twenty first birthday party. I felt the pride course through my veins looking at her knowing I had produced her, she was my blood and flesh. Even as I type this now my eyes well up with the pride I felt as I was looking at her, my offspring. At the time of this dream I did not have kids, these feelings I experienced in the dream I had never had before.

I have had dreams where I am in another life in the future, with the most instantaneous knowledge on everything I could possibly need and want to know. I have had dreams where I was with other dream characters trying to solve the equation for simultaneously existing on more than one dimension at once. I have had dreams where people teach me how to create thought forms and pass knowledge onto me about technology that today we are nowhere near achieving, at least from what I know.

These dreams have changed my life, for I have become content, there are no material possessions I need that I cannot encounter in my dreams. I am content for I know when we die we will continue to be conscious. Your soul will continue to exist, you will continue to exist. Now I know how important it is to become conscious before death. Hence, to stay conscious in life twenty-four-seven even in your dreams.

Developing this content and inner working has also showed me very strange and dangerous things. I have seen beings from others dreams, I have witnessed the subconscious minds of others, even when they are trying to hide information from me. I have seen both demons and angels, the bad and the good. I have witnessed demons trying to pull me off the bed, with my heart beating so fast it feels as if it is going to explode, upon awakening I am in a deep sweat physically. This I cannot explain.

Due to the experiences I have had with my dreams, I do believe we are all connected. What I do in this life to you will determine our interactions in the next life. If everyone could become more aware of this perhaps the world might become a better place. I aim to ensure all my experiences with people are now positive. Imagine a world where we could tap into infinite knowledge, imagine what we would achieve.

I believe all of us have the ability to dream. I have never met one person who has never dreamt, and those that tell me they cannot dream soon come back to tell me they did indeed have a dream sometime later.

This is because firstly to see something you need to be aware of it, then when you spot it, you see it. If you are not aware you will not notice when you see something. Being awake is the key to all dream control. If you start to awaken to your dreams, I believe your whole world will open up to you and you will have wondered where you were all that time.

After you start to learn to dream and become aware of your dreams, your dream recall will improve dramatically. The more you train your recall, the more you will start to become conscious in these dreams. This consciousness will lead to you being able to control your dreams.

Once you have developed this practice you will be able to consciously project your consciousness at will, this is known as an Out of Body Experience (OBE) and there are many people out there that teach about this topic.

As a young girl I had many spontaneous OBEs, at the time I did not realize they were rare and a taboo topic in conversation. All my life people have commented, without me mentioning these topics and spirituality, that they thought I was from another planet in general without any reason. Imagine what they would think if they read this book, they would think I was from another universe.

I was raised in a family that from the outside appeared normal but, on the inside, we believed life was not normal. Both my parents were not in the slightest religious. However, both believed in the paranormal and the unexplained, they would discuss various experiences but yet did not dive deeper into the brilliant experiences they had. They did not choose to go deeper nor to investigate their dreams.

When I was born my father named me to symbolize wisdom. Throughout my young life growing up father would instill into me that pain was simply in the mind, everything was in the mind and having that knowledge allowed you to control fear of the unknown. Why is it that the unknown gives us so much fear? Why do we not want to tackle it more? Why do we hide from it and brush it aside?

As a young baby my father would read me books on memory and having the best mind in the world. He had the ability to control energy and would be able to heal family members with his hands although he told only a few.

Mother had an interest in psychics, tarot cards and astrology as such would look up planet signs for everyone we knew. The tarot cards my mother had were not ones of pictures of characters and drawings of earthly objects or beings, but universe ones with pictures of deep sky objects from the universe such as nebulas. Once she wanted to ask the universe through her cards a question. She was given the answer, however she did not like that answer, so she asked again. She got the same answer. She was angry and asked again. She shuffled those cards for a while and drew out her cards. Again, she was given the same response. This freaked her out and she did not ask again.

Again, like father, mother would not discuss this aspect of her life with anyone outside the family and would almost deny it. Even in front of her partners.

When it came to OBEs my parents both have

developed the ability to project consciously out of the body in their early years. Mother as young girl, perhaps around seven to ten year of age, had a near death experience (NDE) where she saw her life flash before her eyes. Whilst out on my grandfather's speed boat she fell into the sea and nearly drowned and saw her short life flash before her eyes.

After this she developed the ability to astral project, she would look out of her bedroom window at the houses down below and go into a trance, this would then trigger her OBE and she would start flying above the houses, enjoying the view.

This would result in her being known as a dreamer in her school years. Interestingly, in this same bedroom she would wake up screaming reporting seeing a man, my grandparents would frantically search the house and find no one. Nearly forty years later and my auntie would move into that same house. My cousin would start to report seeing the same man in her room and would wake up screaming in terror. I often wonder whether something followed my mothers' astral body back to that room waiting for her to travel out of it at night. Trapped there in that room.

Father had a keen interest in martial arts and meditation, all of his life. He would start to project his consciousness out of his body at a very young age just like my mother. He viewed this as his way to escape the horrors of the world. In later years whilst mediating he would consciously be able to leave his body and would explore the environment around him, walking around the structures he could see but never travel that far.

My grandmother on my mother's side had a near death experience (NDE) when she nearly died from an infection. She reported seeing herself on the bed. As she did, she felt at calm and at ease, peaceful. She was greeted by a close family member. It was not her time to leave this world.

Another time when my grandfather's brother died, the same night he died, she reported seeing him at the end of the bed, stood there watching my grandfather. She has also seen her dad when she has been in pain.

My auntie on my father's side sees things before they happen, she can tell the future of people's lives. We have a deep connection as if she is one of my grandparents too, perhaps she was but in another life.

Speaking of past lives, my auntie on my mother's side feels as if she were my mother in a past life, she would see me every week when I was little and was dumbfounded when I met her boyfriend at just 18 months old and would scream and throw things at him. He reported being terrified of me. I wonder if he did something to her in our past lives and I recognised his soul. His son, my cousin ironically my auntie says we could past for brother and sister we are so alike in personality. We get on like a house on fire, laugh at the same things and think the same way, yet there are ten years in difference between us in age, and we only started to hang out in recent years.

There have been other people I have encountered too that when I met them for the first time, I cannot explain it I just have this connection with them. An instant 'I know you', we just click. These are people not from my home city but from countries far and wide, Thailand, Canada, Japan, China, Africa, etc. How can it be that people from such different backgrounds we can connect with so intensively?

I cannot explain it, but I just feel both my parents were my best friends in my previous life. I feel we were in the military together. Ironically, both myself and my father did try to enter into the military in this life. He was denied from joining the marines as an engineer due to color blindness and I failed the medical for the army due to having a medical history of migraines.

Recently I tried to reignite the flame in my family to gain their interest in dreaming and the subconscious mind. My mother was not interested, and father used his ability to create an island and have a girlfriend experience. Until he realized he needed a physical girlfriend.

My aim in life is to get to the same level as my father who can consciously project and control his consciousness. However, I go through phrases in my life in which I go deep into study and meditation of the spiritual then years without practice and study of it. Life after all, does get busy, at times.

I have had an interest in triggering OBEs consciously throughout my life, but my interest always comes and then disappears.

This interest suddenly came back when I had given up trying to project and simply just started to focus on my dreams for the first time in my life after my roommate in Australia told me I slept talk.

As a result of starting to become aware of my dreams for the first time in my life I started to track them. This led me to create my own dream journal (ISBN: 978-1730811401). I started to modify it to enhance my dream recall.

Next, I started to instead focus on my chakras, for the first time ever, after a month I had the massive OBE, the one I discussed at the beginning of this chapter where I entered into the superconsciousness.

This reignited my interest in astral travel i.e. OBEs and I started to try to continuously project again and monitor my dreams even more.

Having a huge interest, I wanted to hear and read others experiences and what I learnt was a lot of OBEs I had had but had brushed off as dreams were actually a lot more important than I had originally given them credit for.

Reading others accounts it became apparent that a

lot of these accounts I personally would had classified as a dream, incorrectly. I was underestimating my experiences. This led me to decide to share my own experiences for there may be others that underestimate their experiences as I did.

Throughout this book I have highlighted my dreams in the following way to ensure the reader understands when I am referring to the dream world:

> *This format will correspond to the dream or astral world.*

Therefore, when you see the above format please be aware, I am discussing a dream.

Some of these experiences you might not believe until you have your own. I understand that, as an example, I did not believe in sleep paralysis until it happens to me. I want to share a quick story that demonstrates this. Both my parents reported seeing a ghost in their young twenties, in an old Victorian house they lived in with my uncle. Upon telling my uncle he ridiculed them, he did not believe in ghosts.

A few years later my uncle would soon change his mind when he reported going to the kitchen and turning around to see a figure of a man stood in the doorway. It was translucent and just staring at him. Absolutely terrified he closed his eyes and walked through it. This changed his views on the unexplained. Hence, sometimes we must experience these things to believe. I hope you get to experience all you need to believe for yourself.

Furthermore, I really hope you enjoy the read!

1. My Background

I was born with my eyes wide open, not crying, just silent and staring at the whole scene around me. My parents found my open gaze bizarre. I just stared at everything taking everything in. Having been born, two weeks overdue, like most first born children (that seem to be born past their due date), perhaps this is the reason for my curiosity. I simply was waiting to get out into the world and see that around me with my eyes being wide open.

However, for some unknown reason I would not drink anything, this alarmed my parents especially when the nurses had to force tubes down my throat to force feed me. Perhaps I had been born and realized I had been reincarnated again into this life and as a result was deeply disappointed.

Maybe, this is why many new borns come out of the womb crying, the thought of living life all over again for us all. Going from the peace of the spiritual realm into the harsh reality of the world again.

My parents have pictures of me at only 18 months old, sitting on the sofa holding a pen which I was using to color in between the lines of a drawing book. Family would report me as an "old soul", more advanced and aware of the world than I should have been at my age.

Apparently, I was a highly advanced child in my early years, resulting in my parents expecting me to be on a course to becoming a child genius. But that is another story and unfortunately one that would never come to fruition.

At only two years of age, I would encounter my first Out of Body (OBE) experience. Not realizing until decades later the importance of this event which always only felt like a traumatic memory until discovery this was in fact an OBE, not a memory.

2. The Trauma of My First OBE

Just over two years of age, I would witness my pregnant mother in our home going into labor my younger brother.

From my memory I simply only remember the trauma and shock of my mother being in pain and panicking, her waters had broken but I was too young to understand. I remember her being in pain and being helped down the stairs towards the waiting ambulance and being driven away.

My grandmother tried to pick me up as I ran after my mother crying for her to come back as I didn't know where she was going. I tried to run after the ambulance, I could see my mother inside it, in pain, I was looking down on her, but it moved to fast for me to catch up with it and I was left in the middle of the road alone watching my mother disappear. I was deeply upset where my mother was being taken, I did not understand this pain.

As I got older, I would often reflect on this first traumatic memory of mine and be in shock that I was allowed to run after her, and how had I been able to run so fast.

Then one day I was discussing this memory with my mother who informed me that as she was due to leave the house to get into the ambulance my grandmother picked me up and kept me inside.

Due to how much I was crying due to my mother being in so much pain, everyone thought it would be best to keep me inside and not left me outside, nor see the ambulance. I did not get to run after her as I did not even get outside.

How was it then that I was able to see outside, how was I able to chase after the ambulance? I clear as day remember that memory of running after her, looking down at her from above in the ambulance.

Seeing my mother being taken away and "running" or floating after her and being ignored was highly traumatic for me, hence why the memory always stayed with me. I was always convinced I had run after her.

Only years later after learning about OBEs it is not apparent that this was not a physical memory but an astral memory, a memory from my astral body. It was my astral body that had followed her.

My brother was born, and a year later my parents would be going through hell trying to figure out what had happened to him. Years later they would discover he had autism.

During this time to ease the pressure on my parents my grandmother would have me every weekend. However, I would end up battling my own troubles when I would lose all my teeth due to rot from drinking too much blackcurrant juice.

This would result in me missing school time to be taken to speech therapy for years due to having no teeth to talk. Although I was missing a lot of school and getting bullied for my speech, I would still be achieving grades two levels higher than average.

One of those bullies was my friends' mother who would delight in ridiculing me in front of her three daughters. She would get her youngest who was three years old and say, "Look she can speak better than you!". She was an evil woman, during this torment I would just shrug her comments off.

Eventually she stopped her daughter being my friend when we moved to big school through demanding she be put into another class. With what I know now I feel pity for her as more than likely she will be re-born to experience the pain she inflicted on me; she will have to experience not being able to talk just like I was not. Karma.

3. The Nightly Spin of the OBE

Since my birth, my father would read me books on anything related to enhancing the mind. Upon growing older he would teach me tricks, one of these included how to self-hypnotize my brain to improve my mind.

The self-hypnotism he taught involved the following: Every time I went to sleep should tense every area of my body, one limb at a time, holding for a count of between 10 to 20, to both physically relax my body and mind. I would start off at the toes and work up through the torso followed by the fingers up to the arms and shoulders, and then the head and neck. I would hold each part as tight as I could then relax. After this I would feel a tingling throughout all parts of my body and focus on increasing this feeling.

Once my body felt relaxed, I was then to count down in my mind from one hundred to zero. During this count, every ten or five seconds I would tell my subconscious that my mind was entering into a deeper and deeper state of relaxation.

At this point I would then tell my subconscious that I could achieve anything that I wanted. From this technique, I remember numerous occasions where at the end I would suddenly feel like I was spinning around. I would feel as if I were flying around in a tornado.

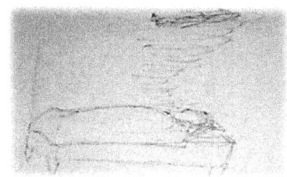

Illustration 1 Spinning Around shows the feeling I would feel, like a tornado, as I would go into a deep state of relaxation.

This feeling would develop so strongly and vividly I would feel as if I were spinning above my physical body. This would result in deep panic over the feeling and I would pull myself back into my physical body to cause the feeling to stop. After a slight alarm, I would relax again then I would go to sleep.

I never did discuss this feeling of spinning with my father and did not even consider it anything until I started to hear other people's experiences and through reading books.

This is how I discovered this experience was known as the 'vibrations stage' of astral projection or an OBE. This spinning feeling is reported as being a sign that you are about to leave your body and are entering into the astral realm. Other signs of this vibrations stage I would go through also included intense heat and high-pitched buzzing sounds.

Interestingly, my auntie's husband who I was discussing astral projection with one day mentioned when he was a young teen he would swell up to the size of his whole room. This would scare him back into his body. However, if he ignored the fear, he would be able to project out of his body and control his surroundings.

Therefore, it seems the trick is to be able to break past the fear of these feelings, then you are into the astral realm. If you want to investigate this more then I recommend a search on the term: astral projection vibrations stage.

However, not all projections have a vibration stage. My mother reports staring out of her window and then suddenly finding herself flying, no uncomfortable feelings prior to the projection. I believe this as sometimes, as I will talk about in later accounts, I would suddenly just pop out of my body. My consciousness would shift, whilst other times I feel as if my body is on fire, I have a strong high-pitched ringing in my ears, and my heart about to explode.

4. Acting Out Past-life Memories at Night

My grandparents took me and my cousin on holiday to Spain, a peaceful holiday with us staying in the same room. My grandparents stayed in a double bed and my cousin and I stayed in bunkbeds. My cousin was on the top bunk and I on the bottom.

One night however my grandparents suddenly awoke to shouting. I was out of bed and using the bed as a type of protection, I was shouting that the enemy were coming and for others to shout at them.

Illustration 2 Acting Out a Past-life Shows the action I was undertaking in my sleep where I was using the bed as a defense against enemies as if I were in a war.

This confused my grandparents who witnessed me then get back into bed as if nothing had happened. I was very young at this time perhaps around 6 years old.

In the morning I was asked about this but apparently, I had no recall of having done this.

Now this is interesting as years later, 20 years later, a flat mate would complain I slept talk as such I would record myself and I picked myself up saying, "Shot them! Shoot them in the forehead, just shoot them". As well as these recordings which appear to be myself directing some invisible army group, I have always had dream of being in the army where I am a guy.

Tied in with everything together when we are younger, we are more likely to remember our past lives especially when we sleep. I believe given all the odd sleep talking and dreams I have about shooting people on the frontline as well as military dreams. I believe in a few of my past lives I have been in the military.

These dreams could be past life memories which given an experiment was recently set up by scientists studying rats where they replayed the same cells to reply memories ten times faster than the actual experience. This showed the brain can go forward and backward and is capable of compressing time as well as the ability to learn from experience reevaluate and compare different experiences.

The ability to rewind or fast forward memories is what our brains can do, and robots cannot. There is a misconception that a dream during REM brain activity looks different. Memories are not compressed in time they are played out in real time as if they are happening.

Brain rhythm shows if someone is asleep however as far as the brain of the individual is concerned it is in REM sleep awake. Non-REM as stated above is more primitive and takes memory and experiences comparing and learning using the hippocampus to involve recognizing where you are acting as an anchor.

Based on this perhaps these are memories from past lives that the soul brings back into the brain.

5. As Above so Below

In my teens after my father and mother had divorced, my brothers and I would go to visit my father some weekends. One of these weekends perhaps my father took me to get one of my ears pierced. However, I had not eaten anything all morning and as such my blood sugar level would have been low.

I remember going in and sitting on the coach in this piercing shop. The piercer pierced my ear, it did not hurt, and I started to walk out of the room. As I walked out of the room towards the waiting area, where my father and brothers were waiting, suddenly I was floating above the street.

I was floating above the street, above the same shop I had been inside, seeing everything from up high and. I could see all the streets around, as if I were a bird high up in the sky hoovering. People below were walking everywhere, they looked so small. There were cars everywhere, as I was looking at the busiest street.

But then I saw my father, my brothers, and myself. We were chatting away walking home. I was mesmerized about how I was so high up in the sky, but yet, I could hear everything we were saying. I could simply zoom in on us all. Not only this but I was in awe of how I was able to be in two places at once. High up in the sky but also down listening to the conversation.

I was below on the ground walking with my father and brothers yet at the same time I was up high in the sky. How could I be below and floating above? As below so above?

Only after writing the sentence above did I wonder about the link with alchemy the fact that the hermetic order mention "as above so below" is this in relation perhaps to us having an astral body that watches us above? A double, that is always floating above?

Whilst I was there floating up high and looking down on myself, I knew this person walking below was myself, but I did not feel like I was with myself, I was this person floating above her. I was the person up in the sky, I was one of two, but whilst up in the sky I was part of one half, I was different to my other half down below.

I was an outsider.

With this weird feeling I decided to go closer to my below self, I was curious.

As I started to move closer, all of a sudden, I suddenly was pulled back into the ear-piercing room, I was in the waiting area, laid on the floor. My father, brothers, and the piercer were all around me asking if I was ok.

This was immensely confusing for me, how suddenly was I able to be in a different place to where I had just been. I was vividly up, as clear as day, up in the sky looking down on everyone and everything as well as my own self. But now I was in a room with my brothers and fathers.

Due to this confusion my first words were "Where am I? How did I get here?" I genuinely had no idea how I had ended up on the floor of the room I was in. It took a few minutes for me to recover my memory and the piercer explained to me I had fainted.

This was an out of body experience in which I saw into the future, I saw my father, brothers, and myself walking home. Yet I had then drifted into the past to where I was currently.

I often wonder if this is why people say, "Where am I?" after they wake up from fainting. Perhaps they had travelled out of the body and being somewhere else, peaceful, and vividly to then suddenly be awoken and pulled back to the physical location causes great confusion and utter shock.

6. The UFO

When I was around eight years old to my upmost astonishment, I discovered that I had another brother, four months older than me. This moment of discovery was one of the happiest days of my life. My brother would stay at our house every weekend and we would discuss the nature of the universe.

One day my brother and I were talking whilst sat next to our autistic brother on the PC. I was looking out of the window of the room which overlooked our city. Suddenly, I noticed some odd lights high up in the sky acting in a bizarre way.

These lights did not look like conventional aircraft due to the unusual symmetric formation, and I just instinctively felt these lights were different.

The lights were made up of around several lights in a certain shape, I think they were a square. I simply remember them being in a formation at the time. All I remember now is being fascinated that the lights were in an odd formation, and so many of them, which was just perfectly still, just hovering in the sky.

I turned to my other brother and calmly said "Is that an UFO?" whilst pointing towards the window with a questionable by confused voice.

He replied instantly, not to be ridiculous, but as he looked over to the sky as he said it his face went white. We ran nearer the window and watched as the lights jumped instantaneously to one side of the sky and over to the other side of the sky, then back to the original position.

We simply were so shocked we did not say anything to each other and proceeded to run down he stairs towards my parents screaming about what we had witnesses.

Upon telling our parents what we had saw they reassured us that we did not see anything. As such, we never spoke about this incident again until over 15 years later when I spoke to a friend of mine.

Illustration 3 The UFO *Showing my brother and I witnessing the UFO hovering in the sky. The UFO floats above the direction of the city's nuclear submarine location, with lights in a type of a formation style. It would instantaneously move from the right side of the sky to the left side and back into the middle in speeds that seemed impossible.*

That friend of mine I was having a discussion with on why he did not speak to his mother, amongst other reasons, he stated that she had claimed to see an UFO and he found it embarrassing. I asked the details of this UFO sighting, and I was in shock to learn it was around the same time of the sighting my brother and I had seen.

His mother would be reported upon in the news for her sighting, she was adamant on what she had seen was an UFO. I asked him where the sighting was, and he told me it was over the city's nuclear submarine area. I asked my father if the same location was visible from our window, and it was. Our window overlooked the direction of the nuclear naval base.

This was shocking for me, as I had ignored this experience and thought it was simply just something normal, and not a UFO. However, after hearing more people's stories in recent years and watching UFO hunters on the History channel, it seems like my brother and I possibly did see an UFO. It seems to be that indeed for what ever reason UFOs are reported hovering over nuclear sites.

Unfortunately, all the effort that my father put into my subconscious mind, and training me to become a good student, would go to waste when we moved to another country to live. Over the next two years my school life would be all over the place and eventually my parents would divorce.

By the time I returned to full-time school my personality had changed. I was a different person, no longer wanting to learn new things, and I just wanted to play the PlayStation or go out and party. I went from being the first child in the infants that owned a computer in the late 90s, being interested in electronics, and learning to code and create websites, to just wasting time hanging out on the street and drinking, not learning anything.

This is one of the biggest regrets of my life about not continuing to focus on electronics and computing at this age. However, I believe this happened to awaken my spiritual side. When we have developed so well in past lives, it makes sense that we need to quickly catch up on emotions and experiences both good and bad again to become evolved and awakened.

Perhaps re-experiencing all that pain in a very short burst at such a young age happens to us so that we can then quickly move onto what is important and develop our consciousness faster.

7. The Spontaneous OBE

Another spontaneous account of many that I can clearly remember vividly was in my later teenage years one day. It was a hot summer day, and I had a doctor's appointment to attend.

I again had not eaten as the appointment was in the morning and walking all the way to the doctors in the blazing sun had left me feeling dehydrated.

The doctor appointment was for an injection. Previous, to this incident, I had no phobia of needles. However, after the experience this would change, I would spend the rest of my life with a phobia of needles.

My doctor called me in from the waiting room, as I walked in, I was asked to stand up for the injection. The doctor proceeded to inject me.

Suddenly, I am at home, talking to my mother. We are having a clear as day conversation about the shed at the side of the house. This felt real, I felt physically back at home. I could see everything just like normal life and the conversation was just as normal. There was no sign of this not being real.

A few minutes into our conversation I was suddenly pulled back into the room with the doctor. Due to the sudden change in environment I was feeling confused as I did not understand how I suddenly was at the doctors when I had been having a conversation with my mother at home.

I asked the doctor, "Where am I? How did I get here?". The doctor explained that I had collapsed upon the needle hitting my skin. This led to a phobia of needles for the rest of my life, which I never had before.

This was an out of body experience in which I went into the future into a conversation with my mother, I know this as a while later I had déjà vu when we were discussing the shed.

The two experiences I shared were two experiences of many times I had spontaneously projecting out of the body. Throughout my youth I would constantly faint at school due to heat and have similar experiences. I was also prone to migraines and violent nose bleeds throughout school.

The nose bleeds and migraines were investigated but the doctors never found a cause for it. The migraines would be so terrible I would have to leave school and try to go to sleep due to the pain and lack of sight. Daily medication did not help control the migraines which I took until my early twenties but can off due to the lack of improvement. In my life I have probably lost around easily 180-365 days to just suffering from migraines.

Oddly, I would always have nose bleeds at least once a month, more often in my pre-teens. Extremely bad nose bleeds that would last well over thirty minutes, this persisted and eased up in my later teens and eventually stopped to some degree in my adult life.

During my school years I had an interest in the paranormal and astral projection however this was shut down by two occasions. One was during a discussion with my physics teacher who told me not to project out of my body as it was dangerous, he knew about it but was fearful of it. He was my favorite teacher and I always had a natural talent for physics especially after receiving 100% for an exam I did not even revise for.

The second was a bunch of retired people that I was randomly speaking to outside a community hall one day, I asked if they knew about astral projection and they told me it was evil and to stay away. I decided to take their advice. This would be until ten years later when I started to regain my interest through dreaming.

8. Father's Near-Death Experiences

Studies have shown that the brain never naturally shuts off, only whilst either under Anesthetic or an induced coma, however, both are unnatural states. Therefore, naturally, unless we die studies show the brain never shits off.

The brain actually 'reboots' itself to consciousness after anesthesia. Research (Hudson, et al., 2014) has shown the brain when anesthetized must pass through certain "hubs" on the path back to consciousness with the activity spontaneously changing its activity as the brain tries to find its way back through a maze of possible activity states (Irwin, 2014).

A mechanism has been found responsible for rapid arousal from sleep and anesthesia in the brain. There is a neural circuit between two brain regions called hypothalamus and thalamus which have been associated with EEG rhythms during sleep. The activation of this circuit signals the termination of light sleep. Hyperactivity of this circuit may cause insomnia whilst hypo activity maybe causes the opposite hypersomnia. The power of this circuit is so strong that activation causes the emergence from anesthesia and the recovery of the consciousness.

My father has died more than once and has on multiple times but been brought back to life through induced or self-induced methods. During these times he reported seeing different scenarios, one pleasant and one not pleasant.

The pleasant experiences of dying for him would happen when his heart would stop. He had heart block which meant that as a super healthy active person his brain would just switch off his heart. As such he would collapse and die, however, the brain would then restart, and he would come back to life.

When this would happen, he reported finding

himself in a white light with a feeling of peace and calm.

However, one time someone killed him, he had an attack on his life, someone had tried to murder him. At the hospital, the doctors were frantically trying to bring him back to life but were not winning the battle. After trying for so long he was pronounced dead.

Upon giving up they and pronouncing him dead it was reported that a few minutes later he suddenly in a split of a second sat straight up in bed wide awake. He shouted out and then collapsed. With a fractured skull, eye socket, and huge swelling to the brain they had to put him into an induced comma so they could open his skull to let the swelling subside.

He had come back to life all by himself. He had started his own heart and had regained consciousness after the doctors had give up. It was not his time at the moment to died and he was not going to give up.

Before he woke up in the hospital bed, whilst the doctors were trying to bring him back to life, he recounts that the place he ended up was cold and empty, with feelings of despair. He said it was unlike the times when his heart had stopped with a peaceful feeling, this was a horrid darkness with no hope.

9. Discovering Dreams

In 2012 I moved to another country, whilst living in this country for 6 months, I shared a room with two others due to the little money I earnt. Living in a shared room with people leads you to discover a lot about yourself you had previously never known about. One of these discoveries was discovering I talked in my sleep, a lot.

At this point in my life I had no real spiritual interest in anything. It had been nearly ten years since I had even thought about spirituality, my mind was focused on developing a career and survival, especially now where I was living paycheck to paycheck.

Some weeks the decision would be on whether I would eat breakfast in the morning, or do I use the money to catch the bus to the train station. A 60-minute walk at 5am, followed by a 50-minute train ride to work, and another 15 minutes' walk. Life was tough at this time, I was stressed, to the extent that I developed the shingles which is an illness people in older age usually develop, not someone in their mid-twenties. My body was weak due to the little money I had to buy food and I had lost a lot of weight.

My mentality was being pushed with travelling to and from work taking 4-hours of my time a day and sleep interruptions from those I was sharing a room with. But all of this is another story.

One night my roommate reported that she was talking to me, whilst I was sleeping. I was talking back to her but then she noticed what I was saying was nonsense. She thought maybe I was just losing the plot as I was tired.

This continued until one day she came into the room and I said, "that is a funny ball you have in your hand!". Then she realized all this time I was sleep talking and not talking back to her as she had no ball in her hand.

As a result, she told me about my sleep talking and for the first time ever I started to notice my sleep. I put my phone recorder on that night and sure enough I did sleep talk.

Eventually I stopped recording myself due to some freaky recordings that were picked up. This would include totally different voices, noises, and speaking to people that were not physically in the room.

One night I recorded the delightful message: "F***king life, you wake, you sleep, you do something, ... you die!".

On the opposite side there were recordings where I was apparently speaking to the archangel Gabriel.

Hearing myself put on different voices and make odd clicking sounds and speaking to unknown people saying I see them all the time in the room with me, was simply too much for me to listen to. I was too freaked out, so I decided to be ignorant to what I was saying, then to be aware.

However, in 2013 I moved into my own house. Due to the quietness of the house, with no one around me to disturb my sleep, I started to remember my dreams.

Over the next few years, I began recording them. Writing down the odd one that came into my memory in the morning. This was perhaps once a month at this point but gradually the recall started to develop intensively.

In 2015, I started to really focus on recalling my dreams, through focus, techniques, energy work and meditation. The dreams had started to become more recallable. My house had more of my peaceful energy within it and acted as a sanctuary.

I was reading every book I could find on dreams, lucid dreaming, astral travelling, and out of body experiences.

In dreaming there are different levels of self-awareness that you can achieve, this is known as your level of lucidity. The levels can vary from fully conscious, where the dreamer can have total control of the dream (also known as lucid dreaming), to no control, and the dreamer simply remembers the dream upon awakening.

The less we are in control within a dream the more the dream is like watching a movie. If we can start to increase self-awareness within a dream to the same level of control as we would in waking life, we would have the ability to control the dream.

The aim of recalling your dreams is to take you gradually from no control/no awareness to full control/self-aware. As you start to remember your dreams and track key themes you will start to alert your brain to recognize you are dreaming leading you to then control your dreams.

Therefore, it is important to learn to become aware of your self-awareness within the dream, so you can start to build up an idea of just how self-aware you are.

The following dreams you will read feature all different levels of lucidity. If I am referring to a dream you will see the text in this format:

This format will correspond to the dream or astral world.

10. The Psychic Workshop

One day my auntie asked me to ask my friend if he wanted to go to a psychic workshop, as he was my friend, they both wanted me to come along to break the ice. Unfortunately, I did not want to attend as I was not interested in psychic workshops. However, they convinced me when I dropped them both off to join.

We had to sit in two circles, one inner circle, and one outer circle. The trainer did a protection prayer. I did not listen to any of it not taking the class serious at all. After the prayer we all had to sit in front of someone and take in turns to see what we saw.

The technique was to calm our mind, imagine we were walking up to a field, seeing a gate, opening the gate, then walking through the field. We then had to imagine we were sitting down at a bench and describe the person coming over and communicating with us.

All the people I sat opposite I had nothing come into my mind and what they would tell me did not relate to me. The last lady in the circle however was different.

Sitting opposite this lady, I closed my eyes and went to the bench. A guy came up to me with blonde hair and blue eyes. He was stocky and had an aura as if in the military he sat down next to me. Telepathically he communicated to me through flashing me images and feelings.

He input into me the knowledge that he loved this woman, but she had broken his heart, he showed me a valentine's heart. He was incredibly sad she did this to him.

Next, separate to him I saw a woman who was being beaten up by a male in darkness, followed by numbers of a year a few years before the current year at the time and a month.

I opened my eyes and said to this lady I could see

a short stocky army type guy that said she broke his heart and a valentine's heart. She confirmed that she knew who it was he had died a few years ago and she broke his heart when she was 16 years old on valentine's day. She said he would always randomly call her every few years, but she would ignore him. She also confirmed he was in the South African army as they were both from South Africa originally.

Illustration 4 The Bench *Shows the bench that I would visualize and speak to whoever would come and sit on it. In this case a South-African that was in the military in his younger days.*

After this I was reluctant but due to the success, I told her the next part about how I had seen a woman being beaten up by a guy and the month and year I saw.

With this she started to cry, loudly, it turned out that her daughter had been murdered by her boyfriend at that month and year. This lady was so overcome that the leader had to calm her down. People started shouting at me for telling her what I told her. My auntie was shouting back at them. All hell broke loose.

I never went to any spiritual groups after this experience.

11. The School Teacher

A friend of mine reported being psychic. Seeing spirts and communicating with them.

One day he reported there was a spirt in my house that did not like him being in the house. He did not want him near me, I too had seen a spirt in my dreams but did not tell him this.

Some of these dreams were quite intrusive where this certain guy would try to have sex with me. This dream I always found odd as I extremely rarely ever had dreams that featured sex and the ones that did featured this same guy. I also at times would feel as if someone was watching me in my bedroom.

I told him to draw this guy he kept seeing and I would do the same. I closed my eyes and tried to feel this spirit. I drew the spirt that I could see, we compared our pictures and we had drawn the same man.

We research the location the flat was over and it turned out that there was a school right where we were. However, it had shut, and the old school head teacher had just disappeared. The old black and white picture showed the man we both drew.

I was convinced this man had been murdered and therefore his spirit haunted the area as he had never been found.

12. ET Contact

Another odd experience that happened one night. I knew this happened and was not a dream within a dream because my partner at the time was there and witnessed it too.

I had started reading about a remote viewer called Ingo Swann whom it was reported worked for the USA government. Unfortunately, he has died now but there are a few books and videos of him in circulation.

One of the videos I was watching featured him discussing how he was able to communicate with aliens. Listening to this I was very skeptical. However, I was hoping for a little excitement if it were true. As such I meditated and thought of any ETs out there.

I said in my mind that if aliens did exist and they were on this planet I would very much like for them to come and make contact with me and have a conversation with me. I put these thoughts out, imagining the thoughts travelling all around my local area. Then that was it I thought nothing of it and actually laughed to myself thinking that I had done this. That night I went to sleep thinking no more about it.

Ding Dong! My bell rang, sitting straight up in bed having been awoken from the bell in shock I thought did I just hear my bell. In the 5 years I lived there I never once had that bell ring unless I was expecting someone.

The bell was hidden so unless you knew it was there it was hard to find, as a result I rarely if ever had cherry knockers. Not only that my house was like a fort you never knew it was there, delivery drivers could never find my house.

I woke my partner up and asked if he heard that bell, he stated he had but to go back to sleep and ignore it. Angry at his ease of which he brushed off the fact someone had rang the bell so early in the morning I got up myself. A few minutes had passed since the noise as I was in such panic by it.

Scared I slowly creep to the window. Looking out I could see someone in a hoody walking from my gate back to their car. This person sat in their car for a few minutes and drove off.

Illustration 5 ET Contact *Shows the man I saw walking back to his car with his hood up on his hoodie.*

The odd thing about this incident was this person only pressed the doorbell once. If I were to travel out of my way in the early hours of the morning to wake someone up and they didn't answer the door from one press of the bell, I would press it again.

It never happened again.

Now I thought nothing of this until a few days later when I remembered that I had asked for alien contact.

At this point of which I remembered I had indeed done this I wondered if that had been an alien coming to have a conversation with me and hence their politeness in only pressing the bell once. To this day I do not know who the hell it was.

13. The Old Marble Pillar

My father was demolishing an old convent that most recently had been used a medical testing facility. The building was huge with at least 50 rooms, there was even underground basements that had been cemented over. The grounds were huge.

Father had reported seeing shadows in the grounds and inside the building in the corner of his eyes. He had always been able to see or sense ghosts.

One day he had taken a lady friend back to the building and when he got up to go for a wee was horrified to see an orb floating towards him. My cousin too had seen things, he had previously ridiculed my father however, one day he did see an orb himself and videoed it. He never went back into that building.

There were lots of stories from the buildings past and builders that had worked there had reported seeing all sorts of things including objects moving and shadows. Some of the builders refused to even work on the building site.

Three different types of owners had lived on the building all with different purposes, apparently the orphans that died there over a hundred years ago had been buried in the grounds.

There was also a massive rat problem.

The building drew lots of different types of people, people that were into dark magic would turn up illegally during the night and carry out spells. My father would turn up in the morning to find satanic drawings and signs on the walls and floors. Lit candles and other odd things, even blood on the floor.

I saw some of this stuff with my own eyes, I went to walk around the building. It was huge, the corridors were huge, there were lots of hidden passages and interesting rooms. But the place gave me a horrible feeling.

One room was the warden's room, from it he could look out on the whole grounds and see everything from up high. It was an amazing view.

A lady turned up one day and was telling dad the buildings history. She had grown up there and stated the building was evil, she claimed bodies were in the garden buried and the people that lived there had been evil and cruel. She made lots of claims and this gave my father the creeps.

One day my father was removing the marble pillars as everything had to clear. One of them snapped as such father gave me part of one of the marble pillars that had fallen off. I put this pillar in as pride of place in the entrance of my flat.

Whilst I was walking down the stairs one day, I decided to read it. I put my hand on it and I could feel over a hundred years' worth of stories. All the positive and all the negative stories.

I will not repeat what I saw as it is private to the pillar, but it was very interesting. The pillar I believe protects my living area, so I want to respect it.

I have always been this way. I think it is important to respect the unknown and mystical. I never respect authority but always the spiritual. My friend once was playing an Ouija board with her friends and family I walked straight out I respect spirts too much to mess around with them.

During the time that follows I started to really recall my dreams and sometimes would start to remember up to five dreams in one night. These dreams were fantastic more exciting than movies.

I would look forward to going bed at night to see what dreams would appear in my mind.

Therefore, the following dreams are from over the next two years that I have picked from hundreds.

14. A History on Sigmund Freud

APRIL 04, 2015

I decided I would start to seek to understand dreams more as such I started learning about Sigmund Freud and his views on dreams when one night I had a dream that featured this knowledge I had been reading as if to test me:

In my dream I was in a pub drinking with a friend and their clever lady friend. The lady friend asked me about Freud as my friend had exclaimed that I was an expert on him when I was not.

Although initially panicking I managed to control my emotions and stayed calm reciting exactly word to work what I knew that movement about Freud.

As I relay lots of information on Freud I was saved as the bar tender came over to tell us we were shutting. I still had one full drink of Black current, vodka and soda water.

This dream was bizarre as my memory allowed me to view exactly everything that I had read about him in the physical. There was so much information that my subconscious had held from the book I read.

The interesting part was that before I was asleep I could not hardly recall any of the information.

However, upon waking up from this dream I could remember more of what I had read and then recited in my dream. This shows that our mind holds onto all types of information.

Unfortunately, as I write this now the information has gone from my brain as if it is something you need to upkeep to keep the information there.

When you are remembering your dreams you will start to notice this and I cannot stress how important it is to develop your dream memory and your waking memory to retain all the experiences and knowledge you learn from your dreams.

Nicola Tesla as I mentioned in the introduction credited his inventions to the dream world. He stated he was able to carry out the experiments before undertaking them in the physical. Likewise, his rival Thomas Edison Science would sleep in short burst and write down new ideas from his sleep.

Srinivasa Ramanujan in his short life of 32 years produced nearly 4,000 items in mathematics of which he reported using dreams to develop his creativity.

The famous Albert Einstein credited his Theory of Relativity and The Speed of Light discoveries to dreams.

15. You Can Die in a Dream

APRIL 05, 2015

Yes, you as a dream character can die in a dream... but eventually you wake up. I experienced dying in a dream, from my readings I have read that apparently you cannot die in a dream. I disagree as I have experienced it on many occasions. If you die you usually either wake up instantly from the dream or else, you will linger, and you will float around for a while and eventually wake up.

The following dream gives an account I experienced of when I died and then woke up:

I was in a house and a man was trying to get inside to kill everyone. I could telepathically talk with this man and was trying to calm him.

Somehow later the man got in and he poisoned us all, we all died. I woke up.

My other experiences where I have died in a dream but not woken up instantly as documented above include the following:

I was held captive by some bad people, eventually I managed to escape from them.

As I ran outside looking for somewhere to hide to catch my breath, I noticed there were a group of people crammed into a small white car, these people were unrelated to the bad people. Just other dreams characters in the dream.

They drove straight at me running me over. These people were just as bad as the others with no respect for life. As I lay there on the road dead my spirit started to float above my body on the ground and I followed the people in the car.

I was very angry with these people who had killed me and carried on watching them for a while, until I woke up from the dream.

In the dream I was able to see my dead dream body and went from walking and running to being able to float. This was a weird sensation. Eventually I did wake up from the dream.

Therefore, when people say you cannot die in a dream I disagree, physically you cannot die in a dream, but your dream character can die in a dream.

Another dream around death featured seeing the afterlife and where we might go when we die tying in with the Greek tradition of the ferryman. See "**The Afterlife Ferry**" dream.

16. Beautiful Astral Realm House

MAY 08, 2015

Sometimes in the astral realm we can create the most beautiful houses that would be of wonder to an architect to deconstruct or gain creative insight from. The following dream features a beautiful house I had the pleasure to live in for a while in a lucid dream:

I was living on the astral realm in a beautiful house where everything was surrounded by water. The house was exquisite with every room having water flowing through.

To travel through the house, you did not need to walk you could simply jump into the water and float to the room you wanted to go to.

Whilst I was there, I was consciously thinking to myself how beautiful the house was and how relaxed I felt there. A sense of inner peace from the sound of the water.

Hours and hours went by and I just enjoyed living in this peaceful house, viewing the water flowing all around me.

Some random people came and started swimming through my house. Extremely angry by their trespassing in my space I started to lose my calmness and woke up instantly.

In my dream I was aware of the beauty of the house within the dream and in awe of the structure and detail. I did not want to explore the dream further or interact with anyone as I just wanted to appreciate what I could see in the dream world or astral realm before I knew it would disappear.

As I was conscious, I was aware I could not swim as such I imagined armbands to wear. It was a great enjoyable dream in terms of appreciating the dreaming landscape and I wonder if people that construct property could use dreams like this to test out ideas.

17. Telepathic Dream Classes

MAY 24, 2015

Sometimes dreams will be teaching me various ESP abilities one such dream I had featured being taught how to have a telepathic dream with someone whilst dreaming:

I was in room with colleagues, but we were in a school environment. We all started talking about dreaming and I suggested to one work colleague that we should try to dream together though cosmic consciousness.

My colleague agreed and all of a sudden, we were dreaming the same dream and communicating telepathically to each other.

Not only were we able to use telepathic communication but we were able to make our other colleagues do things like answering questions.

The head teacher came in and told us off for abusing our skill. This was an odd dream as I was dreaming in my dream and the dreaming, I was undertaking was ESP dreaming. The colleague that I dreamt with was not someone that I spoke to however it was someone that I am sure has ESP ability.

I wonder if we all undertake this type of training

whilst we dream. It is odd how self-proclaimed alien abductees report being taught things by alien races, perhaps they had a dream like mine where they are being taught. I personally have never been abducted by aliens therefore I do not know what these people see. However, I have had many teaching dreams and the content is always focused on development of mankind.

There have been numerous examples of people that have learnt or invented things from their dreams, Nikola Telsa one of the most important scientists in the world due to his inventions around electricity would report that he would be able to invent in his dreams.

Others have credited dreams to their discoveries such as James Bore who discovered the atom in a dream. Thomas Edison believed he received his best ideas during dreaming and would let his subconscious mind control his dreams to find solutions to problems.

People have been more creatively in their dreams using it as a way quite often giving plots for stories. Mary Shelley had a waking dream and created Frankenstein, James Cameron dreamt the story for the terminator, and Robert Louis Stevenson created Jekyll and Hyde in his dream.

18. Comets Hit the Earth

JUNE 18, 2015

I have had a few dreams where there is chaos happening one of these included a comet hitting the Earth:

I was in a school environment when I noticed comets in the sky. Shocked I pointed these comets out to the teachers and my fellow students.

The person I was sat next to started to run outside with me. We ran to my 4x4 and started to drive out of the city. There were checkpoints to stop people.

Something happened and I was on the outskirts alone in a massive warehouse. A lad sent nuclear missiles at me from another warehouse, but I quickly re-programmed a robot to reflect them.

The lad came out of the warehouse and started fighting me, we ended up fighting in the stream.

This dream had although featuring comets they did not hit the Earth.

19. A Telepathic Reptilian Enemy

JULY 03, 2015

There have been a few dreams I have had that featured very strange beings, one of these included a reptilian alien:

Something happened, I do not remember what exactly, however, as a result we had to kill. I knew this bad guy had done something incredibly bad. We hatched a plan to trick him. The plan would involve myself coming face to face with him to trick him.

I went into the room, where he was sitting on a chair and started to speak to him. As my gaze reached his eyes, I realized that his eyes were unlike human eyes. His eyes were reptile shaped eyes even though he looked human with black hair and blue eyes. He was wearing a suit.

As I scanned him with my eyes from top to bottom, I could see all his energy, his energy was not good. However, whilst scanning his energy I realized he was able to read my mind and scan me as I could him.

I realized I was in dangerous as he was going to kill me, due to this realization I quickly escaped before he could kill me.

This was a bizarre dream due to the fact I was

telepathically communicating with a type of being I have never seen before. The odd part was how I was able to scan the energy field and instinctively know that this being was bad.

Illustration 6 Reptilian eyed man
Shows the man that I was trying to trick in the dream. He looked human apart from his reptilian eyes.

In addition, this dream felt like it was in another world, perhaps an astral one where different being can interact. However, this felt as if it was part of my job to catch these type of bad people as if I were an undercover police officer.

20. The Mythical Area

JUNE 19, 2015

Sometimes physical places we know of in the real world can have hidden areas in the astral world:

I was watching something at cinema in school. The film finished I started walking home.

Upon walking out of the school, I came across a man who I asked to try and uncover a covered up mythical area. He helped me scale the wall.

As I got over the wall and looked down, I could see a beautiful area of plants and flowers with a small lake and other weird and wonderful things. It was like a secret garden with a boarded-up back door to stop access from the outside.

Interestingly this area was always a wall I walked past on my way out of school as a child, I had no idea what was behind the wall and always wondered. The wall had a boarded-up door.

It is interesting that my mind chose to turn this unknown area into such a beautiful space as well as the fact that in my dream something triggered me to investigate this space. Could perhaps this be part of my subconscious filling in unknown areas of my past or perhaps I experienced part of someone else's astral world that they had created and as such I had no part to help create hence why there was a difference in style.

21. Drunken Astral Realm Encounters

July 01, 2015

Stories I have read on people astral projecting often report people that they see in the astral world that they know in the real world as appearing as being drunk in the astral world. I experienced this one night when I saw my partner at the time, who did indeed appear drunk:

In my dream I met my boyfriend at the time, this boyfriend however appeared drunk. I asked him if he had taken drugs due to this drunk appearance. He stated that he had not. I was unsure of his response but carried on travelling with him.

We went to someone's house to seek shelter. However, my boyfriend was still acting as if he were drunk. I proceeded to again ask him why he appeared drunk and repeated my had he taken drugs question. Eventually he admitted to taking drugs. I was not happy and left him alone in the building.

Outside it was not nighttime, enjoying the night sky I started to walk. I was aware that I was on the astral plan due to the environment and type of scenery therefore, I decided to take the opportunity on the astral plan to look for UFOs up in the sky. However, no UFOs appeared which I was disappointed by.

Whilst I was walking, I found a stone outside a lady's house, it was the voice of her dead Dad saying, "Love you my red-haired fox". I saw the lady and gave it to her which made her very happy.

This dream felt and appeared to be in the astral plane for several reasons. Firstly, I had a higher level of lucidity and was aware I was on the astral plane. Secondly, my boyfriend had been wandering around appearing drunk before I came across him. This drunk appearance and behavior are often reported as what people see when meeting others on the astral plane when they are physically sleeping but not conscious in their dream when they are traveling in the astral realm. Due to this unconscious travelling in the astral plane a drunk appearance is seen.

I believe the lady was in the astral plane, stuck there having died, however, the stone was created in the physical world from her real father who was still alive and perhaps had left it on her grave. The stone now appeared in the astral realm due to the intense thought put forward from her father.

There have been reports of people creating astral worlds through the power of thought. My own father was able to manufacture an island in which he would go every day to visit.

I believe the city of Atlantis perhaps was, an astral city in the astral plane. There have also been reports of people in Northern America creating maps of their dreams or the astral world and sharing them to create one central shared map to then meet each other. Therefore, I believe this lady's father created that stone on the astral realm.

Power goes into creation and that power comes from thought.

22. Curiosity into Levitation

August 13, 2015

Dream characters can start to interact with you in your own dream, as if they have their own soul or self-awareness:

I was aware I was dreaming and choosing to interact with the people in my dream. I was the only one who had the ability to levitate around me.

I was levitating past a group of people, when one of the people shouted over to me asking how I was able to levitate.

My reply to him was that I feel like I am out of body in daily life and it's the same feeling now in my dream, as such this was one of the key secrets.

The next part, I explained was how I simply just lift both hands up in a way to grab energy, through pulling it up to create a vacuum. Then twist my hands over and slowly push down against this energy which acts like a force and lifts me off the floor.

I explained that I simply would float for as long as I want. Whilst pushing down my body will take me into that direction.

Initially my lucidity was strong in the dream/ However, as time went on my lucidity started to disappear throughout the dream. When you have these dreams you should be aware of this, the more you enjoy the dream and give into it the more lucidity you will lose.

The lucidity was heightened through the dream character questioning of my levitating ability and me referring to the real world. Due to this character interacting and asking this question I feel this was in the astral plane due to the ability for others to interact and show their own personality.

Two years later, April 28, 2017, the dreams characters would take interest again in my dream abilities. However, this time my levitation had developed into the ability to fly:

I was sitting on a sun lounger outside my family home enjoying the warmth of the sun with family members.

A community officer comes over to speak to me and asks me if I want to hang around with others. I declined. I felt like I hurt him so I apologized for hurting his feelings and said I would show him a trick.

I got up and pushed my hands down to lift myself up. I flew up into the sky and all the dream characters started to stare at me. I came back down, and the person was in shock. He asked how I was able to fly, and I stated because we were in a dream.

He asked my auntie what she thought but she denied seeing me fly, he started to argue with her as she was denying seeing me flying. They both started to argue, and

I woke up.

I knew I was in a dream but was enjoying the sun, I could feel the warmth of the sun so intensively as such I chose not to move and enjoy that dream moment. As such when the dream character disturbed my peace, I showed off my flying ability which then broke the dream. This broke the dream because the dream character portraying my auntie could not comprehend the aspect of us being in a dream.

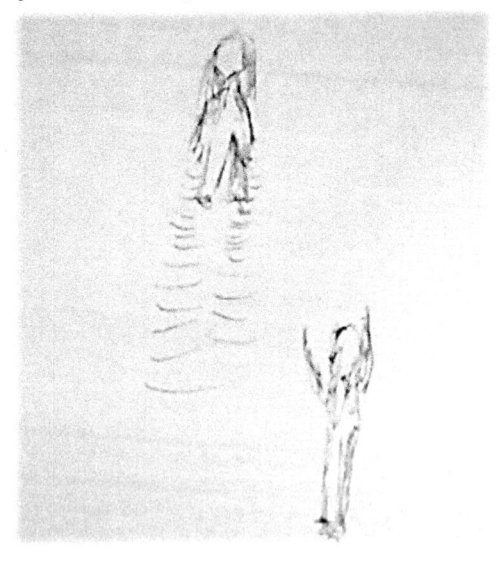

Illustration 7 Levitation Interest *Shows me levitating and one of the dream characters trying to copy me to levitate as well.*

It is interesting that dream characters will freak out when you do not act in the logical manner in which is expected.

23. The Witch

DECEMBER 22, 2015

I mentioned in the previous dream how characters can sometimes show interest in your ability to be able to levitate or fly in ways that they cannot. However, not all dream characters react in the same way:

I was in a dream with a high level of awareness as I was having internal thoughts.

During the dream it was getting late, so I thought I had better fly back to the warehouse in an industrial estate where I was sleeping.

I started to fly back and one of the people around me started to call me a "Witch" as I was the only one flying. The people around me were getting freaked out that I could fly and did not like me having the ability. The people started to get angry towards me flying and started to try to chase me. I flew away.

I think I was in the astral realm due to the reactions of the other people around me freaking out and not being able to fly themselves. It has been noted that when in the astral realm people that are not conscious think, they are in the physical so get angry and uncomfortable when seeing someone defy the laws of the physical world i.e. Physics.

24. Survival Instinct

SEPTEMBER 11, 2015

One of the most utterly bizarre dreams I have had featured a being which seemed to be from the future:

I was walking towards work when an unknown guy offered to give me a lift. I refused as I simply did not trust him. He persisted until I eventually got in the car.

He started to drive the wrong way. I said, "This isn't the right way!". He ignored me, fearful of his intentions I started to talk about survival instinct.

He stopped the car and suddenly got out. He gave me a gun and said he thought based on what I was saying I might be "the one". He told me I better start to run, I did, and we started to shoot each other.

He had an advantage as he had a machine that allowed him to re-heel his body. This device was a telepathic healing device.

My survival instinct kicked in. I pretended to be dead. As he walked over, I quickly managed to shoot him and get his device. I started to heal and shot him more.

Eventually I telepathically gained his helmet and gun.

I won and killed him, it felt great but when he shot me it really hurt.

In this dream, the guy was acting as if it were his mission to destroy me and the only way, he could do this was through my dreams.

The technology was extremely advanced and worked through mind thoughts and not physical precision. The talent of controlling the device laid in the thought of the mind and not in the strength of the physical body.

When you dream dreams with such advanced technology try to recall as much as possible that you remember seeing about it. What did that technology do and how did it work, and what differentiated that technology in the dream from the technology available in today's world.

25. The Superconsciousness

SEPTEMBER 24, 2015

In 2015 I split up with my partner that I had been living with for over a year and a half, for over the last year I had been trying to get out of the relationship but because he was so lovely, I felt guilty to leave him. However, our relationship was passionless, he was more like my brother, not a lover. Eventually I managed to break free and I was extremely happy, joyful, I felt immense happiness in my life of being free from him.

During this time, I had been practicing energy work on my chakras for thirty days straight. This would involve focusing on each chakra spinning around for a few minutes each and then energy coming down through my body. This would be over a 45-minute time period.

I would start with the base chakra imagining that area being red and spinning around for a few minutes, then I would move up to the sacral chakra, imaging the area being orange and spinning, then I would focus on the solar plexus chakra picturing it being yellow and spinning around. Then the heart chakra being green and spinning around, followed by the throat chakra being light blue and spinning around, next the third eye chakra as being dark blue and spinning around, and finally the crown chakra being purple and spinning around. Next, I would send energy down through me.

After this I would do another full cycle followed by a focus on the heart chakra visualized as a lotus flower in a pound.

Then I would do a cycle of the chakras again but with the chant to each. After this I would then focus climbing a pyramid and looking up at space.

This whole sequence would last 45 minutes and at this point in my life for the first time I had completed this routine for 30 days straight.

In September 2015 I awoke one morning, very early and dehydrated in my flat. I went into the kitchen to drink some water then climbed back into bed and fell asleep:

I wake up but instantaneously feel confused as the ceiling is closer than usual to me. However, I had spent the last year reading everything I could on Astral Projection and knew if I were to have my next OBE to stay calm as this is what pulls one back into the physical body, as such I stayed calm.

The instinct in me was that I was having an OBE, I continued to tell myself to stay calm and not to get excited nor to look down at myself in the bed as I did not want to get pulled back into my physical body. My awareness level of consciousness was as waking life. I was fully aware and conscious.

As I calmly looked around my room, I could see that everything was shiny and clearer compared to how everything looked in 'normal' life in the physical.

In the corner of the room there was a solar system, it was bright and drawing me towards it. I decided to float towards it, as I was floating, I felt like I was just consciousness I did not feel I had a body as I had in my other OBEs.

Upon floating towards the solar system in the corner of my room I found myself floating out of Earth, out of the orbit, it was becoming smaller, now I was floating out of our solar system.

I am then floating out of the galaxy and finally I am floating through the universe with galaxies floating past me.

At this point my consciousness was so strong, stronger than waking life. The feeling I had at this point was so brilliant there are no words that can describe what I felt, this feeling was fully euphoric, peaceful, and calm all at once. I knew everything possible to know but at the same time nothing. My knowledge was infinite and my feelings supreme.

I just wanted to stay in this way, stay where I was. This continued however, as I was fully conscious and lucid, I thought I had better get back to my body so I could remember everything and write this all down before I lost consciousness.

Suddenly, I am back on my bed, but I was aware I was still out of my physical body. However, this time I could feel my astral body. As such I decided to roll out of my body towards the left off of the bed.

I tried to shift my astral body off of the bed it moved but I did not feel as if my body has hit the floor it just rolled and stayed floating on the floor. Once on the floor I did not know how to move so I tried to crawl in my astral body using my elbows. This was a weird experience.

After managing to crawl into my front room I was then perplexed on what to do next. I decided to call out for my neighbor's cat.

She came to me but as a kitten. I stroked her for a while and then started to get tired losing lucidity.

At this point I started to lose control of my consciousness and enter into a brief dream which resulted in two dream characters trying to kill me in my flat.

One stabbed me with a knife and I suddenly awoke upright in bed. I remembered everything.

When I woke up, I was feeling fantastic, refreshed, and totally alive. I was in awe of what I had seen and felt, the most amazing out of body experience I have ever had. My energy felt fantastic.

Upon walking into work one of my colleagues who was able to project out of his body at will and had shared many OBE experiences with me came straight up to me and said, "You projected out of your body last night, didn't you? Your glowing.". I was surprised by this and any doubts I had about his experiences faded away as he could physically see my energy was different. He had never said this to me before.

This was the most intense out of body experience I had ever had with different levels of consciousness.

The feeling I had I actually could not find a word in the English dictionary to explain the feeling. Upon further research after this experience the only term I could find to describe what I had experienced was "the Superconsciousness" discussed by Nikola Tesla and Karl Jung along with the words Euphoria and infinite knowing of everything.

After this experience I started to recall my dreams more, up to five dreams in one night.

26. The Beautiful Iris

NOVEMBER 07, 2015

Some of the dreams I have had feature some incredible odd sights when looking at myself in the mirror within a dream:

I accompanied a colleague who wanted to buy a tent, he wanted me to hook him up with my old school friend. Agreeing to this we both made our way to her house. My friend answered the door and agreed to come camping with us.

The next moment, my colleague simply vanished, my friend and I tried searching for him, but we could not find him anywhere. My colleague's boss rang, who happened to be dating my friend, saying that he was dumping her.

We both found this phone call weird and instantly thought maybe he had kidnapped my colleague.

I was now with another colleague walking and having general chit chat. A storm started with constant massive thunder and lightning above us in the sky. As I pointed at the weather above us to alert my colleague to the weather all the power disappeared around us.

We carried on walking and made our way to the gym, which was on the edge of a beach, the tide was really low.

I went to the toilet and was not impressed with the quality. As I looked at myself in the mirror and into my eyes, I could see inside my iris were all different multiple colors of blue, green and brown with swirls in them. As the tide went out a Mum and her kids ran around the unseen corner.

Surprised by this I called my colleague in to look at my eyes.

As the dream shows the mirror image looked different to waking life. There were beautiful colors and the iris was the most mesmerizing aspect of the reflection, it was as if all the true colors that are naked to the human eyes in the real world were suddenly visible in this world.

27. Levitation in Force in the Astral Realm

DECEMBER 2015

I have noticed that when I developed my lucidity, I would start to gain the ability to levitate:

I was working with a bunch of criminals doing jobs earning shed loads of cash.

I found myself relaxing in the swimming pool and then levitating through the air. I was aware I was the only person that had the ability to levitate, it felt natural and good.

The guys came to get me then we did a massive job. The guys escaped with money as per our plan.

Illustration 8 Levitation in Force *Shows me levitating amongst other dream characters in a room which had a swimming pool.*

This dream was weird as I remember people specifically walking next to me talking to me as I am levitating. I was aware they were unable, but the levitation felt great.

The ability to levitate in a dream feels so easy and natural. You simply bring both your palms up towards you in a sweep upwards motion and without stopping flip your palms. Then press the energy created, down to the ground to then lift you off the floor.

If you do become lucid in a dream try this, you will be amazed at the ease of which you can use this simple technique. As you gain more control over your levitation you with soon start to fly.

28. The Demon Fight

DECEMBER 01, 2015

In addition to the ability to levitate, as lucidity increases with dreams, I have noticed the more I seem to be able to witness demons. They will then try to fight or scare me:

I was in various situations where a demon kept trying to get me, but I kept escaping. I was part demon myself which made me fast too.

I was in my friend's car when the demon tried attacking again. I was fighting with the demon trying to get it away from our car. Eventually I fell off the car and was fighting the demon on the field.

I killed it.

I seem to sometimes be able to have the same strength as them. Another dream I had demonstrates this.

Everywhere I went this demon would appear. I was with friends and this demon kept trying to fight me.

We were driving down the road whilst I was fighting the demon. I had the same powers as the demon I was half demon, I was fast, I could fly, and I had the same strength.

In the end I killed the demon.

This makes me wonder if the demons in the astral realm can spot souls that are more lucid and therefore, try to attack these souls to frighten them out of the astral realm.

The fact that I have had dreams where the characters notice I can levitate further adds credit to this theory in being noticed with a higher level of lucidity.

29. A Beautiful House

JANUARY 18, 2016

As mentioned before the astral realm allows the most beautiful houses to be created with very interesting.

The rooms are always different sizes compared to how they seem to appear form the outside. For example, you walk through one door which you assume leads to a tiny area and the area is huge. The following dream gives a demonstration of this:

A beautiful house with a massive corridor of which led to huge rooms. I went into one room which was four times as big as a sports hall which was my bedroom. It had a shrine to a goddess.

There was a room which was a kitchen but looked like a restaurant that overlooked the whole of the outside. Outside was an escalator to leave the house.

My Mum turned up to see the house and told me to hide my bedroom and to make the rooms look smaller to avoid jealous. As such she helped me to put in place fake walls so that people could never see how big the house was.

The interesting aspect of this dream was the scale, the corridor did not seem big enough for the space of the rooms.

30. Secret Room to Another World

FEBUARY 14, 2016

Sometimes I have noticed that the buildings in our dreams can feature portals to other worlds:

I was at my current house getting ready to leave, I left the house to go and meet someone at an event.

We were about to leave the event when we decided to eat first as such we went to the canteen. I said I was not going to eat chips as I didn't like them and didn't want them. I then proceeded to go back to my house.

When I got back to my house the door had been kicked open. However, nothing had been taken but the carpet had been taken up.

I called the police. The police couldn't find anything.

My friend from earlier was there with her kids, I said I am going to kill who ever has broken into my house.

My friend said. "don't say that around the kids they will think you're talking about them". My friend left and everyone went.

I was looking around my house. I went pass my bedroom and a corridor suddenly appeared, this led to a room I had not previously ever seen.

I walked into the room and all I could see was a wall in the middle with cupboards in front and behind. Behind the wall was a window. I found this so odd that a secret room had appeared.

On the floor was a hatch as such I lifted up the hatch and it led to a block of flats.

I realized that what had happened was someone had come into my flat through this hatch. I was quite happy I had another room to add to my house.

I started moving things onto of the hatch so no one could come in through it. I went to the location the hatch led to which was a shopping mall.

There were steps leading to the hatch, so I started pilling lots of wood to block it.

Someone had their car covering the latch so I put a massive block of steel over the hole. I said to the old man he could move his car back over the steel.

Then some people came including a lady who sung beautifully. I said her singing was beautiful.

This dream was interesting due to the portal in the hatch that took you to another place. The portal looked normal with no haze or glare just another area.

31. Fighting in the Astral Realm

MARCH 28, 2016

When you fight in the astral realm it is like you are Bruce Lee. The gravity helps you to fight beautifully, feeling every hit:

I am with my father who is walking and I am on a bicycle. We are going through a park and some people on bikes start to chase us. A few try to grab me, so I brake suddenly to make my back wheel go up and knock them out.

Then we ran into a building, through into a room which we bolted. Dad smashed in a window so we could escape.

This bad person comes in, so I elbow him in the face and spin around to knock him out with another elbow and follow through with some back fists to the other people. Dad and I escape.

Next, I go into the cinema where my work mates are waiting for me as I am late.

Whilst fighting I was having internal thoughts of where to position my body and which defense would be the best. During the fighting I was enjoying the feeling of defending myself.

My movement was free and flowing as if I were in a dance, every movement was powerful and well placed. The hits were effective and strong.

32. The Afterlife Ferry

MAY 12, 2016

This dream featured a potential insight into what happens perhaps when we die:

I died within my dream and found myself on a boat with my mother and auntie. We were aware we had died.

We however waited on the boat to go back but it never moved.

As we walked around this huge boat, we noticed it stunk. There were rotting people everywhere that we waiting to go back.

As we looked around us there were hundreds of other boats with people getting off them and walking somewhere in queues.

We decided to get off the boat to avoid becoming the same as the rotten half dead bodies around us.

Upon leaving the boats there were signs telling us the directions to walk. It was like coming off an airplane like being in an airport.

The corridors said this was the end of life ready for the next journey. Everyone was queuing. There were signs everywhere saying, "This way".

We were in the "afterlife" and we had just got off the ferry.

This dream was unusual as the place felt like it was the afterlife, and this was the ferryman that certain cultures have talked about including the ferryman of Hades that would transport souls across the river from the world of the living to the world of the dead.

The fact that in the dream the ferry could never go back was interesting as in death we cannot go back to our original life and only into a new life through reincarnation.

In the dream we have the knowledge that we had died and had to keep walking with the group of people. However, I did not get to see where this led to.

33. Feeling Drunk in the Astral Realm

JUNE 21, 2016

There are times when you are not fully lucid but yet aware you are in the astral realm, feeling drunk:

I was drunk. My mate's brother randomly came to collect me to take me back to my city.

As he was walking me back everyone kept looking at me as I was only wearing my yellow bikini.

We were talking about spirituality in the car, a place in the city and a major date in a document on the place home page that was majorly important.

I believe due to the fact I felt drunk in my dream I was in the astral realm. Often when we are in the astral realm people will appear drunk unless they are fully conscious, the same can be true that we will feel drunk.

I was not fully conscious but aware that I felt drunk. As such I believe I was given a message. When I searched for the date I was given and the location.

I was expecting to find nothing as I was not aware this place had hosted any events, however there was an annual Buddhist event on the date I was given.

Could it be my subconscious saw this event and brought it to my conscious self via the dream or perhaps someone tried to tell me on the astral realm.

34. Meeting Great Grandmother

JUNE 27, 2016

Sometimes we can have dreams where we meet our ancestors, people we have never even met. However, they are not guaranteed as being the nicest soul's as this dream of mine demonstrates:

I was speaking to my great grandmother who was telling me that she did not like my grandmother. Angered by this statement, I questioned her reasoning. She could not justify it.

I turned her rude opinion back around on her, stating perhaps she was the one with the problem. She looked like a witch with a hooked nose and long hair. I was not going to let her talk about my grandmother in a negative way.

I believe I probably did meet my great grandmother (on my mothers' father's side) in the astral realm. Interestingly, my grandmother did report this lady treating her with contempt, which she never understood the reason for.

People often report dreams where they see loved ones that have died or spirts that they later find out resemble those of their extended family that they have never met.

Someone from a different country once reported to me (upon meeting me for the first time) that one of my ancestors was around me, protecting me. Specifically, my great-great grandfather on my father's side with a name I had never heard of was given and as a result I disbelieved this medium. The medium insisted this man was around me, describing how he appeared and even describing the dog by his side and the dog's name.

Later, I verified with my auntie her grandfathers name, she did indeed confirm the name and even the description of the dog and the dog's name.

Thousands of years ago Shamans and our ancient ancestors would report speaking to ancestors through their dreams and passing on the knowledge they were given.

Quite often there have been reports of people seeing spirits when they have died, often upon awakening from a dream. Young children will often report seeing family members that they have never met. Could it be our ancestors watch over the family?

People often can see family members of others not in their own family. My grandmother reported seeing my grandfathers brother stood at the bottom of the bed watching over my grandad after awakening in the night. That was the evening he died. She states if was if he came to say bye to my grandfather.

You can see accounts of this from first responders on a TV series called '911 Paranormal' where first responders report seeing the soul or ghost form of a person that has just died when they are first at the scene of the death.

I think it is very important to be aware of this as if we unfortunately do encounter the death of a love one then we should remain open incase they do choose to come and say "Bye", or perhaps to come and say "Hi" every so often.

When my mother needs help, she reports asking for a sign from her beloved auntie that she was close to and unfortunately died at a young age. The auntie she reports will give her signs in the form of a white feather to signal she is there watching her and listening.

35. The Buddha Event

JUNE 2016

Dreams sometime show us things to act upon however sometimes due to the shock we do not always act on that which we should:

I was told to check out a certain city website for a specific building, in this building was an event on a certain date and it was extremely important for me to attend this event.

I woke up and found this dream strange as I thought the building was just a church. When looked at the website for the building it was randomly holding a one-off annual Buddhist event on the date I was told.

This freaked me out a lot and unfortunately, I did not go to this event and have regret not listening to my subconscious mind.

36. The Beautiful Celesite Crystal Drawing

JULY 09, 2016

Sometimes dreams can feature the most exquisite artwork that is impossible to image, the following shows one of my dreams featuring a beautiful drawing:

Someone I lived in the same apartment with told me I could have their crystals. I snuck into their room to collect them, I tried to be quiet.

However, there was an unknown person there, she had hold of a drawing someone had done. She said it was too plain and had to be better. It was a valley with trees on either side, a bright sun in the top middle part.

This gave me an idea for my picture, so I went to find paper.

I drew a beautiful crystal (Celesite) on an altar surrounded by roman pillars. The crystal was in the middle and two pillars on either side.

Waking up from this dream was odd as I woke up hot and was not able to breathe and with a sore throat.

The famous artist Salvador Dali encouraged artists to use their dreaming state to achieve ideas for their paintings. He reported the idea for 'The Dream Approaches' (1932-1933) coming from a dream.

37. Training Astral Projection and Meditation

JULY 10, 2016

There are many dreams I have where I am teaching spiritual practices or being taught myself. The following is a dream where I was the teacher:

I was training astral projection and meditation to a bunch of people in a town environment. However, soldiers came and were killing everyone in the town.

I managed to escape with a few others through hiding behind and under vehicles.

The dream was odd as I was teaching people in depth something that I have not mastered myself in this reality. However, in my dream I had mastered the skill and knew everything about how to accomplish astral projection. Hence, why I was teaching others.

I would have another dream a few days later where I would meditate in my dream:

I was sat around a table doing mediation on my dream.

I often wonder whether this practice in the dream helps to develop the ability in waking life.

38. Beautiful Peacock

JUNE 10, 2016

The following features a symbolic dream to do with the development of the energy body. Sometimes dreams will display symbology of which we should reflect on to understand the meaning behind:

> *I saw a beautiful peacock with the most beautiful colors radiating from it. I was walking along the street when I saw it. I was mesmerized by the beauty of its feathers and colors.*

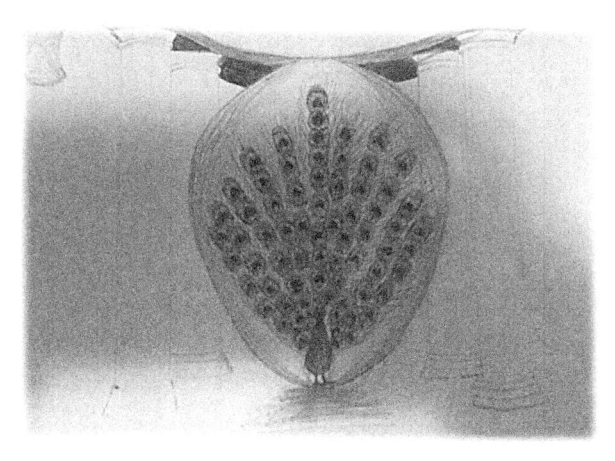

Illustration 9 The Beautiful Peacock *The peacock is in the energy egg, which is around our energy field, the peacock represents in alchemy transformation. The columns represent alignment of the picture to center the peacock to balance both sides of a perspective the ultimate aim of alchemy. This is evident in the moon on the left and sun on the right side of the drawing.*

Seeing this peacock symbolized transformation through energy development of my outer energy body.

39. The Astral Realm Tourist Attraction

JULY 12-17, 2016

We sometimes can have dreams in the astral realm which can take us to very interesting places where we encounter various experiences:

I was driving around alone when I came across a tourist attraction. It was an old town in the desert. Lots of people were there.

I got out and started following people marveling at the buildings. You could go inside the buildings.

One building required a passport. The guy in front of me was saying to his friend he did not have a passport his passport number was blank.

The rooms were very minimalistic.

It was interesting that so many people had gathered in the dream to look at this minimalistic building, as if this were in the future and they were looking at an ancient site. Ironically, this ancient site looked like someone's house from today.

The countries that these people's passports were from I did not recognize. I feel this was a made-up location on the astral realm.

40. ESP of Others' Intentions

AUGUST 19, 2016

Predictive dreams are very common, in particular this dream featured a friend of mine whom I saw he considering a purchase:

A friend was in my dream he wanted a mini tea pot set.

I rang my friend and told him about the dream, and he stated he was actually looking at mini tea pot set the night before wondering whether he should buy a specific one as I had described.

This experience was very odd as I would not expect this to be something he would look at and we had never discussed. He was actually a little embarrassed over this potential purchase.

41. The Desert Bookshop

AUGUST 28, 2016

Reading in the astral realm is possible:

I was in a desert town that took me hours to find. People that lived in the town were able to go to the bookshop, pick up any book, and take the book to read and return later.

The bookshop had every type of book from OBEs to Superconsciousness.

When you read in the astral realm the books are amazing and the knowledge goes straight into your brain. Not only is it easier to read, there are unlimited books that you can pick up to read.

In this dream the amount of books available on such a niche topic was overwhelming and there was not enough time for me to read them all.

42. OBE Whilst Meditating

AUGUST 29, 2016

After my major OBE into the Superconsciousness, I decided to continue to try and project out of the body at will. One night in, I awoke and looked at my phone to check the time. It was 4am in the morning. I started to meditate as I was fully awake and not tired at all.

Whilst I was meditation, I was trying to shift my consciousness a few inches away to the left:

One moment my awareness was in my head and the next minute the awareness had shifted above my body.

Becoming aware that I was floating out of my body, I knew I had to stay calm. I told myself that if I were out of the body right now then I wanted to jump through the wall on my left and out into the carpark.

Suddenly, I jumped through the wall and was floating above my property overlooking the car park.

At this point my excitement was so intense that I was pulled straight back to my physical body.

Perhaps as this happened in the early hours of the morning my body was still tired. However, as my mind was fully awake maybe this is why I was able to project into my astral body out and of my physical body.

If my mind was tired, then I simply would have fallen asleep during the meditation.

43. Entering Someone's Dream

AUGUST 28, 2016

I had a friend who I was able to predict the guessing of thought with. This person did not classify themselves as spiritual yet would always be able to guess what I would think.

The game would involve me thinking of anything in the world, finding an imagine and looking at it on my phone, the person would then guess what the image was I was thinking of. I would then do the guessing. We had over 90%.

One night this person featured in a dream I had:

I was staying in a log cabin in the woods with my friend. My friend introduced me to two older people that came to stay with us for the holiday. One had curly short hair and blue to green eyes, whilst the other one had longer straight ginger hair with a pointy nose. They were both in their late 50s.

The point at which I was introduced was also as I was trying to build a fire in the middle of the log cabin. My friend started to help me with the fire.

I asked my friend if they had dreamt that. My friend confirmed that they indeed had dreamt and asked what my dream was about.

I proceeded to explain my dream and my friend went quiet. I asked my friend what was wrong, and they exclaimed that they had had the same dream. My friend was very freaked out by this and did not speak to me again and kept their distance ever since. I have not spoken to this friend now in years.

Sometimes the truth can be too strong for people to face and those that have a natural gift end up trying to hide it. I had the strongest connection ever with this friend and was terribly upset that the connection was not developed or able to grow.

We must be careful when entering other's dreams as it can be trespassing. One example that I felt very guilty for in 2018 was when I met someone who was very spoilt and came from a very wealth background.

This person was incredibly rude to my closest friend at the time and that day I remember being angry with this person. That same night I had a dream where I was able to break into their computer and steal their passwords to steal all their money. I awoke from the dream feeling a bit embarrassed and told my subconscious not to think in such a negative form.

That same day I saw this spoilt person, I asked if they had a good night sleep very casually. However, I was shocked by their response.

They reported they had not slept well, as they kept dreaming of someone trying to hack into their computer and steal their money. I was so mortified with myself that I could not look this person in the eyes, and I kept away from them ever since. I felt very guilty even though they were an idiot.

Even though I only met this person three times I was able to penetrate into their mind, this was very scary as I wondered if others could do this to myself. Then it reminded me of the film Inception, and I wondered if the director Christopher Nolan had had dream experiences where he entered into the dreams of others and perhaps this is what led to his film.

I would love to speak to Nolan to discuss this further and find out his reasoning for the film. I wonder if he has had shared dream experiences.

44. Re-entering a Dream

AUGUST 28, 2016

People often report of re-entering their dreams:

A few friends and I were in an unknown city, we saw a group of Chinese mafia giving knighthoods to its members.

The police came so the mafia started to roll up all these rugs as Buddha's were praying on the rugs.

One of the rugs I decided to roll up however when I finished everyone had gone. I thought I better hand it back else the mafia would think I had stolen it when I hadn't.

I was trying to find the mafia, but people were getting suspicions why I was looking for the mafia. I speak to someone I know who says he will help me find their building so we can sneak the rug back.

We get into the building and hide in a room as people are walking past. I fall asleep and this guy is gone so I get scared as I don't know my way around the building. As such I take out my Nokia phone and put it on silent, so no one hears me.

As I am going to the stair I get to the basement and realize it is too low so go back up and view the most beautiful duck egg and gold rooms. I spoke to someone and asked how I get out and she sends me to this salon.

Someone asked me if I was this person and I say yes, they think I am the designer, so I go along with it. I try to open the doors to get out, but they said they bolted it to stop people leaving without paying. They ask what I am doing so I state I am checking it is secure.

At this point I physically woke up. However, I was not happy I could not open the doors, so I fell back to sleep and re-entered the dream.

I am back in my dream and I go up to the windows and with all my might they will not open up. I am now panicking as I have exhausted all options to try to escape in this dream.

A lot of people I speak to enter back into their dreams to change the endings. This is the beauty of waking and going back to sleep.

Now if many people have experienced what I experienced in terms of re-entering a dream then why do they not develop these skills to be able to control their dreams. I think this dream symbolizes that we can expand on and develop our dream recall further.

45. False Awakening: Dream Within a Dream

JANUARY 27, 2017

False awakenings when they happen are simply bizarre, they make you doubt yourself and your mind in terms of how something that is not reality can feel so much like reality:

I awoke from my dream and wrote everything down that I had dreamt, the dream was incredibly interesting as such I made sure to note every detail possible that I could recall.

I then went back to sleep and woke up sometime later.

Upon awakening I grabbed my book, I searched for the dream, I was searching my book for my dream but could not find the page that had been written.

I had specifically written down the dream in detail. However, now I could not find this dream that I had written. Frantically I turned through every page looking for this dream. Nothing.

I realized that I had actually written down my dream in my actual dream, not in reality. This was a typical example of a false awakening. I had simply tricked myself through awaking within a dream.

This had happened to me previously to this dream a year or two earlier:

I was being chased by the Japanese Mafia through the streets. My friend had annoyed them somehow and we were not trying to escape from them.

Suddenly I woke up, I was in my friend's spare bedroom, I got dressed and made my way down to the kitchen.

My friend was in the kitchen, I started telling her about my dream, she stopped me immediately and described the rest of it. We were in absolute shock.

We had both dreamt the same dream.

This realization was amazing, and we were both in awe, after a long conversation about this dream and the larger context of reality we went back to our rooms and got ready for the day.

We left the house and started walking down the street.

I woke up.

The whole dream was a dream within a dream. This was unusual as the dream was so long and usually false awakenings are very short. However, there have been accounts of people having woken from dreams then going to work and then waking up, therefore, this is a common phenomenon.

This was possibly the weirdest false awakening that I had had due to the fact that I was able to have a false awakening with another dream character with a focus on sharing a dream.

46. Robot Wars

SEPTEMBER 06, 2016

Often dreams of war can occur in my dreams:

There were robots everywhere as there was a war going on between the humans and robots.

My previous human enemy became an ally to help me fight the robots. Every time you blew up a robot you had to move as it gave away your location. We were constantly on the move.

One robot I blew up you showed the beacon giving off the signal.

The guy I was with was ex-military, so I asked him to help me find my family, he was not keen. He was teaching me escape and evasion tactics.

We came across someone I knew who told us not to leave life regretting those you didn't help or the thing you didn't do.

This got the guy thinking and he agreed to help me find my family.

There was mass panic of emotion throughout this dream.

47. Meeting My Subconscious

SEPTEMBER 10, 2016

Dreaming gives insight into the inner self and challenges. It's quite often reported that people will ask their subconscious important questions and receive answers in their dreams.

These types of dreams are often different to your other dreams and you have an instinct which I cannot explain in that they are part of you:

A stranger turned up at my house as the back door was open, the patio doors would not fully shut. This stranger was trying to get into the house, so I asked him what he wanted and who he was.

He did not answer my questions as he was very manipulative, strong and strange, totally psychopathic in his nature, but his manipulation did not work on me as I could see through it.

He said he wanted me to operate on him and he wanted my brother to turn a screwdriver in his leg whilst I was carrying out the operation on his body so he could focus on the pain.

Before going to bed I had asked my subconscious mind to let me talk to it as such I believe the stranger was my subconscious. The stranger for some reason never crossed over into the house which it was as if an invisible barrier was stopping him.

48. Predictive Dream

SEPTEMBER 14, 2016

Sometimes we can have predictive dreams:

> *A work colleague from another office who I did not particularly like or dislike and had not spoken to in a year came up to me and started speaking to me.*

I saw this guy in the physical world, apparently, he got his meeting date wrong and had read the wrong date and as such ended up in our office and he started speaking to me. I had not spoken to this guy in a year.

49. Predictive Dream: Random Birthday

NOVEMBER 16, 2016

Another predictive dream, an odd ESP experience in which I dreamt of a colleague being hysterical:

> *An ex-work colleague was running around trying to get a present for their boss and asked for my help.*
>
> *I spoke this ex colleagues' boss and mentioned the fact that I had dreamt about a birthday with the ex-work colleague trying to find them a present as such I asked if it was their birthday that day. They stated it was not, however, they mentioned it was their kids' birthday this day and my ex work colleague still kept in touch.*

I never had a dream where this person featured before so perhaps it was my subconscious remembering my work colleague from last year looking for a present on behalf of this person. This ex-work colleague was their personal assistant and continued to be their good friend.

This is another example I wanted to share perhaps demonstrating global consciousness. The ability to pick up on other thoughts without being that close to them is very scary. If this is true than that means there can be no secrets amongst others.

50. Headache Tablets

JUNE 16, 2016

We will often have predictive dreams to warn of us dangers that lie ahead. The following gives an account of a dream I had that foretold a health condition:

Was with a friend and we were trying to find a shop in the city center for her to buy headache tablets.

After awakening from this dream, I met my friend the same day and did proceed to develop a headache and as such we ended up trying to find a shop to buy headache tablets. As such maybe this dream predicted the future, or I had a headache because of the dream.

51. Internal Thoughts

SEPTEMBER 23, 2016

An internal thought can often be as strong in our dreams as normal waking life:

I was with a friend in a princess yacht enjoying the sea when a massive wave, ten times the boats' height appeared.

I had internal thoughts I was going to die and was frantically searching for my lifejacket. My heart was intensively beating.

After awakening from this dream, I was in a deep sweat. My heart was beating heavily. Sometimes our dreams can be so intense that our physical bodies react whilst dreaming.

I have had dreams where my heart has gone from 40bpm in deep sleep to suddenly 180bpm. Often, I will wake up suddenly from such a dream.

If you start to develop internal thoughts in your dreams your lucidity is increasing and you will more than likely, I find, start to notice an increase in the number of lucid dreams you experience.

52. Watching My Friend in Their Dream

OCTOBER 02, 2016

When you start to enter people's dreams you will be able to watch them from afar:

My friend was working on his car when a tractor came and started trying to crash into him. He was shouting for his Dad to call the police.

I could see this from my window so I started to try and dial the police from my phone, but my phone would not work.

I take a picture of the tractor, but it morphed into a massive green 4x4 with 8 wheels. I am trying to write down the number plate, but it keeps morphing.

The next day I spoke to the friend I saw who told me of his dream where a tractor was trying to harm him, and he kept seeing a girl stood far away just watching him.

53. Same Dream, Difference Perspectives

OCTOBER 05, 2016

A shared dream can happen with someone whom you have not had much interaction with. I had spent a few days conversing with someone about dreams and we decided to meet for coffee.

Upon the day of meeting in the morning, I asked him if he had dreamt over the night, as this was the topic of subject for a few nights. He replied saying he had dreamt, and it involved me. Finding this interesting I asked for further detail of the dream.

He proceeded to tell me the dream involved meeting me in a forest, but upon seeing him I ran away. He said he was trying to find me in the forest but could not.

I found this a bit bizarre and considered whether I should still meet him for coffee. After all nothing could really happen meeting someone for coffee in a public place during the day.

However, the most interesting part of this story was that when I got home, I picked up my dream book to see what I had dreamt that night and discovered I had dreamt I met this guy in a forest and I had run away from him. He was trying to find me, and I was hiding from him in the forest.

This was shocking. The same dream but from different perspectives.

54. Morphing into a Bat

OCTOBER 08, 2016

In our dreams we can shapeshift ourselves:

I was at a work event and congratulating someone on his birthday and how he was getting on in life. His girlfriend asked if she could come with me as I was going to grab a drink, I say of course. It is just the guy's girlfriend and I. We see a slide and she say shall we go down it.

We both go down it, but I don't stop at the barrier and go through the wall into another street. There are dodgy people all around, I have no idea where I am.

A street robber tries to mug me with a knife, so I start fighting him, whilst this is happening a guy, I know from another company, turns up and helps me. We end up overpowering the mugger.

We are walking to a similar place, so we start walking together. I end up losing him and pick up another stranger.

When we get back to the event it has disappeared and there are people there. We watch them but then they turn around and look at us. As I panic thinking what will they do or say to me I instantaneously morph into a bat and fly away.

The instant morphing into the bat was unexpected as I had not even expected to have morphed into a bat. Why this animal I do not know, perhaps due to it being dark and harder to see.

This morphing into a mammal was a bizarre feeling as I could feel the wings moving to make me fly.

Another dreams a few months later features me morphing into a chameleon:

I am with a person who I do not know, but in the dream, he is my boyfriend.

We both get kidnapped by a psycho killer who takes us back to his house. We both manage to escape.

I let my boyfriend go first but the psycho killer is about to catch up with us, so I tell the boyfriend to go on without me and escape to freedom.

I divert the psycho killer, and then suddenly hide by morphing into a chameleon and hiding in a pipe.

In this dream I was aware I was about to morph into a chameleon. Perhaps having learnt the ability to morph in the previous dream allowed me to learn how to do it in this dream.

The feeling is odd as you just instantly pop into being the animal that you think of. You still have your mind in the dream it is just the body that changes.

After I morphed into a Chameleon I was stuck, left to get caught as my movements were slower compared to a human.

55. Becoming Lucid in a Dream

OCTOBER 14, 2016

Sometimes when you need help and your lucidity is strong the dream characters will try to help you, this prompts you to gain even more awareness:

I was walking back from somewhere unknown in my dream. I was sat on the floor by my car as I was working on fixing it. When I was getting engrossed, this van with lights off would start coming toward me. I would get internal thoughts of "wow, who is this?"

I became aware of the feeling this was not a nice person in the van and sensed he was a serial killer that wanted to kill me.

As soon as I would run and get into my car, he would drive back to his car parking space in corner. This happened a number of times. He had long blonde curly hair and a beard.

I figured out what was happening, so I went to the city center. I went into a shop in the city center and came across a friend. She agreed to walk back to the car park with me.

The unknown guy was no longer at the car park.

I was looking for my car in the car park but could not find it. I asked my friend why I could not find my car and she replied: "It's because you haven't programmed in your dream to have your car and you need to think of your car without thinking about it.

As the dream still needs to feel real and as the dream knows it is not there that would crack the dream if the car appeared. You need to think of the car without thinking about it. The dream needs to feel natural. If you think of a car when it blatantly is not there it will not work, it will not appear. You need to believe in believing in the place you currently are that your car is there, and this is not a dream."

After hearing this I decided to give it a go and thought in my head "I genuinely believe I am here and not in a dream and my car is in the car park". Nothing happened so I tried again then the car appeared with different number plates.

I got in car and drove off.

I found it extraordinary that the dream character was telling me how to programme dream objects and giving me advice in the dream. My level of consciousness was the same as everyday life.

This shows if you need help you can ask the other dream characters around you.

56. The Beauty of the Dream World

OCTOBER 16, 2016

Dreams can provide us with the most beautiful scenery to witness and oddly we can appreciate it whilst we are simply dreaming:

I was walking down a street and some people I knew offered me to jump in the car for a lift. One of them was eating an ice cream, which made me want one.

They drove me to the beach I was headed. I got out of the car and went to search for an ice cream to buy.

Sat alone on the beach with my ice cream, I marveled at the beauty of the waves, the sea, and the sun setting.

I decided to go and buy a telescope for the dark sky to be able to then marvel at the stars in the night sky.

Perhaps this realization of the beauty of the environment within dreams is what gives artists inspirations for their drawings.

In dreams if we can take a moment out and just appreciate the scene, we will often wake up feeling energized, as if we have physically been in the sun.

57. The Food Drama

OCTOBER 16, 2016

In dreams we can often experience Déjà vu as we can experience in the physical world:

A chef dished me up a plate of food. However, he forgot to heat the food up as it was freezing cold. I complained but then ended up eating the food cold.

I went outside and I realized I had been in the place before in another dream as I recognized the stones and building.

Then someone next to me said I would not be able to help.

I was able to recognize the place before from another dream just as we do in waking life. This is unusual and shows higher levels of lucidity.

58. The Time Machine

OCTOBER 17, 2016

Time travelling devices often feature in dreams:

My brother and I were trying to find my friend's apartment. We could not find it anywhere as such we stand outside a restaurant smoking (even though I do not smoke in real life). I was complaining about smoking saying it felt horrible. I hated the whole smoking feeling but was still smoking.

We went inside and there was an armed robbery going on as such we pretended to be baddies so we could sneak out.

Walking down the street some kids start chasing us, we are running. We are at a water fountain and my father comes out of a time machine and rescues us.

It turns out we went to the wrong time period and therefore we could not find my friends flat.

It is interesting to note how in dreams we can appear to time travel into different time periods. I could have become more lucid in my dream perhaps I could have studied the device to learn its scientific secrets.

59. The Buddhist Book

OCTOBER 30, 2016

Sometimes in our dreams characters can attempt to teach us things about other religions:

I was with a friend who introduced me to his boyfriend which preceded to tell me about a Buddhist book he loved to read.

He started discussing Buddhist law and a table book which applied the teachings.

I am not a Buddhist but admittedly I have never studied Buddhism. From that of which I have heard about Buddhism I seem to naturally follow what is taught.

Given the fact this is not my first dream mentioning Buddhism I have grown curiosity into the religion. However, I do not like to follow a set religion and take things as I experience them to make my own judgements.

60. Men in Black (MIB)

NOVEMBER 05, 2016

This dream was bizarre as it featured the famous men in black (MIB) whether these guys are real or not I am not sure but there have been numerous accounts of people that reported seeing MIB in real life. The TV series on the History Chanel called UFO hunters features an episode on the MIB which witnesses report being threatened:

In my dream I was a famous person that was called Angel. I was in a swimming complex where someone was teaching me how to swim. Whilst I was there a reporter was writing a local article on me.

Later I was driving back with a friend, but my friend disappeared when we got to somewhere, we had been headed. As such I drove back to my house.

I drove through my gates and drove into my usual car parking space. However, someone was parked in that space. I told these people that they were not allowed to park there as it was private property.

The three people in the car got out of their car, they were all dressed in black suits, two males and one female.

They walked up to me, one of the males took his sunglasses off and was staring at me in the eyes. I told him not to stare at me like this else I would stare back at him.

I started him out.

The female went to say something to me as she did, I grabbed her by the throat and pinned her to the wall as I could feel she was about to threaten me. She collapsed and the two males were in shock.

I told them all to get out. They left.

I found this dream a bit odd, and initially thought little of it. Until I started investigating and discovered there are accounts of people seeing the men in black. However, my case happened in my dream the accounts of others happened in real life.

61. The Superconsciousness Task

NOVEMBER 09, 2016

Sometimes we have dreams which feature our daily work, our mind takes us through aspects from the daily or perhaps problems we have encountered. However, I have had many dreams where I am not undertaking usual work but some type of interstellar cosmic work for the universe:

I was assigning people tasks on the Superconsciousness and telling people to go and research parts of it.

This dream was unusual as the work context was beyond my capability of understanding when I awoke. In the dream I fully understood why certain research areas were needed as I had assigned them, however, upon awakening I did not recall any of this and just remembered knowing.

62. DNA Structure

NOVEMBER 11, 2016

Dreams can often show us structures that make no sense and are unlike anything we have seen in the real world:

I was in a DNA structure monument and the stairs were built like a DNA structure. There was a bigger compartment with all plants in and you could look all the way down.

This monument was huge and hid under the sea.

This structure was interesting due to its structure to replicate the visual aspect of DNA. I do not remember the purpose of the structure or why this was under the sea. I have never seen anything like this structure in the real world, nor have I heard of such structure.

63. Soul Group Discussion

NOVEMBER 13, 2016

There are various people that we can encounter in our dreams, sometimes I have met people that I apparently know but yet never met in the physical world:

I woke up in a van which had to be moved. My partner that I was with suggested we go to get food and meet their friend who actually was my friend too.

We met our friend and were discussing soul groups. This guy (our friend) said he was part of my soul group and not my partners.

In the real world I do not know who this person was and got the feeling perhaps I was astral travelling with my partner and the comment the guy made was in relation to being in the astral realm where my partner thought he knew this person but actually it was someone related to me. Hence why the person mentioned only being part of my soul group.

64. Through a Tunnel Whilst Mediating

NOVEMBER 2016

DMT is a substance taken by tribal Sharma's to trigger OBEs. One night I was lying in bed awake when I felt a sudden hard push down on my third eye chakra area. Little lights started to swirl and go into many different shapes, then I started travelling through a tunnel. This was unlike anything I had ever experience and I started to freak out.

I sat up physically wide awake on my bed freaked out as to what the tunnel was. I immediately thought of a certain person and texted them to ask if everything was OK with them.

The next day they admitted around the time I had texted them they had taken the substance DMT and had the trip I described seeing.

Our conversation in the past about OBEs and drugs had crossed as I was not in favor of taking drugs to influence OBEs and create the experience however, he was for them. As such he would never have told me that he was taking DMT, he only admitted to it after I told him what I saw as he was shocked that I had picked up on his actual trip.

As such when he took the substance, I believe I could feel his initial experience though the connection we had developed. I believe I felt his experience of the drug.

I have had similar experiences where people try to hide something from me, and I will see it in my dreams or whilst meditating. One day my dad did not want to tell me he had an argument with someone, but I dreamt about that argument the same night. I told him about it, and he admitted it had happened, but he did not want to tell me.

65. The Negative Entity

DECEMBER 15, 2016

There have been many encounters in my dreams where people try to offer me advice or warn me on issues:

A person was warning me that he had noticed that a negative entity was latched onto my energy field.

However, he stated as I was so powerful the entity was not able to drain my energy instantly and instead was slowly draining the energy as this was the only way it could achieve sucking out my energy.

This dream was freaky, and I did not know what to think of it. I started to focus on my energy field and imagine any holes being patched up. I started to undertake further chakra development. If this was a real warning from a spiritual being than I decided making my energy field stronger and aiming to protect it was all I could do.

I brought a necklace with a crystal to protect me however after a while I felt I did not need this as an amulet and as such gave it to a friend. I believe protection devices should be used like bike stabilizers, used to start us in our development but then no longer used.

For this reason, I do not use any protection equipment or amulets as I believe developing my mental energy is stronger. It is the thought that makes the protection field not so much the object.

66. The Beauty of the Trees

DECEMBER 17, 2016

Our dream can sometimes be so beautiful that even the most common everyday sights can become exquisite with colors and energy that is beyond description:

I was in a dream within a field of which I was living in a caravan, when I became aware, I was dreaming I decided to look around the field and explore. I started to fly by pushing down with my hands which acted as a pressure force to lift me off the ground.

Then I flew to the outer edges of the field to explore. I was struck by the movement of the energy of the trees surrounding the border of the fields. I was mesmerized by the trees marveling at their beauty.

I continued to fly around looking at the beauty of the created field with the glowing of the leaves and bright beautiful colors. The thought through my head was of impressiveness of the beauty of the dream.

After a while I then thought I should check out more of the dream. I started to travel via flight to the only exit point I could see that had a path. Along this path was a street I thought I would go into the buildings along the way.

I entered the first building and was met

with a barrier. I went into a second and again met with a barrier.

On the third building I saw someone hide in a wall. They said, "Ah she has seen us" and they ran off.

I asked why I could not go anywhere, and a voice said I only had one option available I could go back or forward but not off the dedicated path. As such I was being led to an end point. I was not impressed with this and tried every building I could find but they were all blank like a film set upon entering.

I was wondering if this was my dream why could I not go outside of these boundaries. I decided not to change the dream and just go with the flow and see what was waiting for me.

The beauty of the trees and leaves were nothing like I had ever seen. The colors were bright and vivid. Flying around the corners of the field felt free and great.

I had major frustration when I could not go off track. I wanted to explore the dream not just go with the flow. However, I decided to just go with what I was being pushed towards in the dream due to the barriers I kept facing. It seemed as if there was great effort being taken to ensure I followed the dream.

The dream reminded me of the film The Truman Show with the people hiding behind the scenes.

67. Guiding an OBE

NOVEMBER 10, 2016

I was with a friend whom I was attempting to guide into an out of body experience (OBE) through hypnosis. As I talked my friend out of their body they reported being in the ceiling. I asked them to go and meet my spirit guide and ask why I was not able to have more control of my OBEs.

My friend instantly met a skeleton looking being dressed as a knight with all the armor on. His arms were closed, and he was stern looking. He reportedly did not want to talk to my friend and upon my friend asking him the question he telepathically replied that he would not tell my friend anything and that my friend was a "selfish f**ker". I asked my friend to draw what was seen.

Interestingly, I would actually part ways with this friend which would include reasons of selfishness however at the time I did not understand this comment as I thought my friend was awesome.

The being my friend described and drew for me was actually one unknown to my friend that I had seen in my meditations before.

I cannot verify what my friend saw only what I was told was seen. However, the fact the description fitted something I had seen myself and not told my friend about interests me. I had previously experienced this being and he was known to me as the Gatekeeper.

In my experiences with this being he was indeed very moody and always refused to let me through the gate to another realm.

I was meditating one day and tried to project to another place I flew into the sky and went to a portal. At this portal he was stood there and would not let me through. I was not impressed and demanded he let me know however he would not, and some angels came and took me back down and explained I was not ready yet.

***Illustration 10* The Gatekeeper** *Shows the Gatekeeper my friend drew after I asked my friend to ask to speak to my Spiritual guide. Shows a skeleton being with a helmet on and armor.*

The gatekeeper was never rude to me however unlike he was to my friend.

68. The Intelligent Man

DECEMBER 19, 2016

In dreams we can often meet some of the most incredibly intelligent dream characters:

A person was teaching me his knowledge. The knowledge was amazing, and I woke up instantly with great insight. The person was highly intelligent.

After time the knowledge disappears, this is why it is important to write the knowledge down. To this day I have regretted not writing the information down.

However, the intelligence he taught me was so strong I had expected it to stay in my brain however this did not happen. Always remember to write down every detail of the dreams you have. If you find yourself losing some part of the memory of the dream go over that dream again.

There was a time I would be able to get someone to open my dream diary from 2015 and pick a title of a random dream and I would be able to remember everything about that dream. Now I am not as good at this and some dreams I have had I have difficulty remembering but know I had them as I wrote about them.

Dream intelligence and the ability to bring that intelligence and store the memories is a balancing act, just like going to the dream you need to constantly train your dream muscles.

69. The Teachings

DECEMBER 26, 2016

Often dreams can go on for a while when we seem to be being taught as if in a school:

My friend and I were being taught information. The dream went on for a long time and I stated to my friend I did not want to leave the premises, as it was freaky outside.

It felt like we were in another world yet still human beings that had somehow been teleported to undertake these teachings.

My friend found us an abandoned room to sleep in. After our teachings, we would go back to the room.

This dream was interesting as this friend was the one that at the time, I was sharing dreams with, as such it was interesting that we were both being taught in the same school and class. Unfortunately, I do not remember what I we were being taught on but felt extraterrestrial in nature.

70. Continuum of Time & Sleep Paralysis

DECEMBER 28, 2016

In our dreams it appears nothing is impossible to solve, not even the continuum of time and exiting in multiple dimensions:

Someone broke the continuum of time, of simultaneously existing in more than one dimension at the same time.

Because of the fantastic discovery this person was taken away as discovering the Continuum of time of simultaneous existence was illegal.

After this shock I start to walk with one of the other researchers discussing some of our other research.

However, I am walking towards a storm which is huge.

I awake from the dream, I assumed I had awakened however I suddenly see a demon stood next to me. The demon was not happy about me witnessing the dream character solving the continuum of time to be able to exist in more than one dimension at a time.

The demon and I started to fight. I told him that he did not scare me, as soon as I said this, he paralyzed me so that I could not move my body. I was frozen.

He starts to pull my legs off the bed, I am trying to fight against him, but I cannot. I am screaming trying to get my body to move to fight back doing everything in my power to fight. Helpless I call out for my auntie's help, but nothing happened.

At this point the demon started to torture me, he wanted to destroy me and rip out my soul but then the pain and fear was so intense that I suddenly moved, and he disappeared.

My body was physically dripping with sweat all over as if I had been running a marathon and my heart was pounding extremely fast.

The time on my phone showed it was the early hours of the morning around 4am. After this experience I could not sleep. I remembered reading about these types of experiences, yet I never believed in them as I had never had one, this was a sleep paralysis attack.

My heart was beating so intensively during this episode that I would not have been surprised if I achieved a heartbeat of over 200bpm, having achieved over 200bpm whilst exercising in the past.

After having this experience, I did wonder if this is a reason why some people are reported to die in their sleep due to the intensiveness of the fear and the such high heart rate. It is worth nothing that I now own an apple watch which monitors my heart and although I have not had such terrible experiences since wearing my watch, there have been many occurrences where my heart will jump up to 180bpm whilst I am sleeping and a few minutes previous it has been around 40-50bpm.

The trauma of the sleep paralysis took my mind from remembering how the simultaneous existence within more than one dimension at once has been achieved.

The following month I would have another experience of a demon attacking me, this time followed by all my clocks in my house stopping.

A gold watch, pink watch and a clock in the bathroom. These are the only clocks I own apart from my mobile phone.

The gold watch stopped working, the pink watch stopped, and my bath clock stopped. Like there is a magnetic field around my house or something.

In the sleep paralysis whilst we are sleeping, we have a hormone released so that we do not act out our dreams but as soon as you wake up this is stopped. However, some people report that they wake up and are unable to move this is because this hormone is still being released and usually comes back after a short period of time.

Skeletal muscles are paralyzed during sleep by two brain chemicals during REM sleep. REM sleep is where most recalled dreams occur.

In REM sleep the eyes continue to move but the body's muscles do not, this prevents injury. People that have REM sleep disorders act out their dreams as these chemicals do not get released.

This can lead to serious injuries to the dreamer and anyone around them.

71. The Evil Lady

JANUARY 05, 2017

Often the dream characters that are evil within my dreams will end up exposing themselves as being demons when I do not show fear:

I was asleep and an evil lady came in and started throwing spoons at me that woke me up. I was infuriated upon being awoken in such a manner and chased her out of the house.

She morphed into a demon and started to chase me, so I ran back inside and into my mum's bedroom.

I told my mum that a demon was trying to kill me, and I quickly put something against the door to block it. I frantically asked my mum to pass me the phone to immediately call the police, but the phone did not work.

When I encounter an evil character in my dream that are unable to scare me, it is often the case that they will reveal their true form of a demon, as a last attempt to scare me off. I wonder if they expose their true self because they lose power and cannot keep the fake façade they portray. An example of this can be seen my **recent dream** in which a demon revealed itself to me by accident and then ran off, seemingly powerless and in disarray.

72. Seeing a Demon In Another's Dream

JANUARY 09, 2017

This experience was one of the scariest experiences of my life because of how real it felt at the time. Up to this point I had been successfully having scared dreams with a friend, we had been carrying out experiments and were proving very successful in either me appearing my in friends dream watching from afar or actually interacting in my friends dream.

One night I was meditating late in the night, usually I would have been sleeping at this time however, I had not felt tired on this occasion therefore decided to meditate instead.

As I started to meditate, I sensed a presence in the physical to my right. Because of this I stopped my meditation and opened my eyes.

To my utmost horror there in the doorway stood an evil looking being. I could feel evil from this being. The being looked like a praying mantis but blue, black and red in color with claws like razor blades. Describing this being even now makes my eyes water and gives me chills on my body.

On the claws blood was dripping off. I had an intense evil feeling coming from this being that it wanted to harm me.

I could not believe what I was looking at. I closed my eyes, shock my head and looked back. It was still there.

I turned my head to the opposite side and slapped myself on the face to test if I were dreaming. I could not believe what I was seeing there was no way it could be real.

I looked back and this evil being was getting closer. I knew I had to stand up to it so with all my might and all the power I had I shouted at it to go away and turned the side light on next to me on my left-hand side.

This evil demonic being disappeared. I rang my father immediately who told me never to tell anyone about what I had seen. Of course, I ignored him as I knew this was nothing to do with me.

Then next day I spoke to my friend who I was sharing dreams. I asked my friend to write down their dream and I wrote down about the demon experience.

We swapped papers and to my amazement my friend had described how they had a dream at the time I would have been meditating where they were camping and this evil insect looking creature with sharp claws had sliced up the tents. This being was killing everyone in the dream. My friend was trapped in the tent in the dream and then whilst they were being attacked in the dream, they called out for me to enter their dream and try to help them.

Illustration 11 The Demon from a Friends Dream *Shows the demon stood in the doorway of my bedroom as I am on the bed. A tent is drawn on the left to represent my friends dream. Whilst I am on my bed witnessing the evil being.*

After this event I stopped trying to have shared dreams with my friend and I did not experience anything like this again since (touch wood).

I truly believe this being came to me after my friend

thought of me in their dream and because I was in deep meditation, I could see it. Had I not been in a deep relaxed state of relation this probably would not have occurred. I was most probably at the hypnogogic state.

This is why it is very important to be careful who you connect with, if you are to share dreams with others or attempt any type of spiritual practice these people must have no entities around them for these entities can end up around you as happened with me. But as fast as they come, they can go (touch wood). The praying mantis was a pet of mine which I loved so this insect was not a fear of mine.

It is also worth noting that the day after this event three of my watches/clocks stopped working. One clock I had not replaced the batteries for a while, therefore I assumed it was time to replace the batteries.

However, another clock stopped working which has new batteries in and should not have stopped.

Then, the third watch was a mechanical watch that you shake for the battery. This watch I had also been wearing the whole day. I needed to take this watch to a watch repaired to actually get working as it would not respond.

The fact all my watches in the house which happened to be three stopped working on the same day after this incident freaked me out. Whether it was an odd coincidence or something more paranormal is not known.

73. Reading a Book in the Astral Realm

JANUARY 17, 2017

It is reported that you cannot read books in a dream, however, I disagree with this based on my own experiences. I have actually read books covering many different complex topics:

I was strolling down the street with my mother, when we suddenly came across an interesting book shop. I asked her "should we go inside?", she nodded silently.

As we entered the book shop, we saw shelves full of books on the occult. I was amazed by how many books were, and being a novice on subject of the occult, I started to read fascinated by the content.

Whilst I was reading, there was a guy in my peripheral vision giving a lecture on the occult. I was so mesmerized on the content of the book and the lecture that I did not know what to focus on.

I have spoken to many people and read articles where the authors state that they cannot read in their dreams, but my experiences have contrasted with this. In my dreams, I have on countless occasions explored new topics through reading. Perhaps, I am not dreaming, and I am in the Astral Realm and therefore able to retain my consciousness allowing me to read and process information as we do in the waking life.

74. Astral Realm Running

JANUARY 20, 2017

In the astral realm if you do not fly or levitate you can run which feels absolute effortless:

I was running in full control, it felt great. My feet felt light and my body movements were smooth, as if I were gliding in space without frictions and gravity acting against me. Everything was working with me, as if I were in a river and flowing with the current.

I was in full control of a long and difficult run, but run was effortless due to my natural ease to maneuver. When I completed the run, I was left feeling fantastic and energized.

When you run in the Astral Realm, you can feel the energy that is generated within your body. The running feels great because you do not get out of breath or have the ache of real-life running. Therefore, you can constantly run and enjoy the moment.

75. Dream Telepathy

JANUARY 14, 2017

When we are relaxed and calm in the mind our dreams can result in picking up on the thoughts of those closest to us:

I am talking to my cousin in her flat where some thugs try to attack her.

My father shows up with a black eye. Not impressed with my father having a black eye, I suspiciously asked if him and his friend had been fighting. However, they point blank deny any fighting.

Upon waking from this dream, I had intense suspicion of my father being involved in a fight. I contacted him asking if he had been fighting that night. He replied he had not, however, before he had gone to sleep, he had been trying to find a video for a song which featured a video with a guy and a black eye.

Therefore, it seems that perhaps I picked up on these thoughts from my fathers' subconscious mind which showed itself in my dream. This has appeared to have happened numerous times with different family and friends.

Another situation would occur three years later where he would be in an argument with someone I knew. However, in my dream I saw this argument and rang him to discuss what I had seen. He was shocked and knew that the more he would try to hide his thoughts from me the more I would pick up on them.

76. ESP Dream

MARCH 26, 2017

Dreams sometimes can give us glimpses into other people's lives without us communicating with them:

I decide to go and visit my mother. Upon arrival at her house she is annoyed at feathers being everywhere.

Confused as I cannot see any feathers, I ask her what feathers she is complaining about. She insists there are feathers on the floor, but I seem to be unaware of their presence.

The day I awoke from this dream I rang my mother, as it was Mother's Day. I did not mention this dream and just asked how she was in general. My mother starts to complain about my brother coming home from an event and feathers falling out from his bag and going everywhere on the floor.

I believe I saw the feelings that my mother was experiencing through my dream, perhaps through dream telepathy I was able to pick up on the situation. Hence, why I was not able to see the feathers in my dream but able to speak to her about them.

If we were to cross reference our dreams with people around us, I believe we would start to see cross overs and dream telepathy more. Sometimes the thought forms of emotions from those closest to us seem to be able to show up easier in the dream then the situation itself, perhaps demonstrating emotion is strongest for ESP dreaming.

77. Going into the Future

FEBRUARY 05, 2017

Another episode of time travel in a dream:

With some of my friends at a shop with different people from my family. I was eating a twister, but I did not like it, so I returned it.

My friend was there with his dog. We started to walk home as my friend had to meet their partner at 3 o'clock.

I came across some people that were talking about dodgy stuff, two men and one little kid.

I overheard them talking about telescopes I ask if I could buy one and they said no because they were worth 70,000 pounds. Everybody in the street has a telescope.

Suddenly, I am at a futuristic city. I was teleported to the to this place. I am looking around me and wondering where I am.

I started going up to everyone and asking what year it was, they had a look of confusion on their faces and they said it's 2099.

I am in shock as I realize I have traveled to the future.

A few people started crowd around me a realizing I had come from the past they were asking where I had come from.

It seems given the lack of limitations of dreams this often results in the ability for us to past through time. The details of the dream and the differences between the years are always incredible.

Illustration 12 The Future City *Shows one of the buildings I saw in the future city. The building was curved with elongated windows that were huge. The whole concept of the building was circular.*

78. Blanking Out Dreams

FEBRUARY 08, 2017

When dreams are horrific we can programme our mind to block the dreams from our memories:

I woke up wide awake from a dream with a massive jolt I looked at my phone and it was 3:15am and I thought to myself I need to go back to sleep because I have a long day ahead of me tomorrow.

I fell back to sleep and when I woke up, I could not remember my dream, I did not write it down.

I spoke to my friend the next day called my friend whom had a dream in which I was in and I was in trouble and they woke up at exactly the same time as me, they had actually screenshotted their phone too.

Maybe therefore I did not remember my dream because the dream was horrible, and my subconscious mind hid the dream from me due to the trauma. Hence, the sudden jolt to awaken me.

79. OBE After Waking From a Dream

FEBRUARY 25, 2017

Often if a dream is traumatic enough we can use this to project out of our body with the consciousness that we develop:

I was in a Japanese city cycling as fast as I could on a bicycle through the streets to get away from an incredibly evil lady that was chasing me.

This lady looked like a witch with dark long hair and a big crooked nose.

I suddenly awoke instantly with my heart pounding. However, my legs were still moving as if I were still cycling.

I realized that I was floating out of my body carrying out the movements in my astral body.

Having realized I was in my astral body I decided to take the opportunity to astral travel so I naturally without thought started to cycle my legs as fast as I could and was catapulted through my ceiling of my room and up into the sky above me.

I am now floating above my city looking down at the landscape. I was in awe of the view, a satellite view of the city from up above.

This started to excite me and as a result I

was instantaneously pulled back to my physical body.

This immediately woke my physical body and I sat upright in bed with my heart still pounding over my dream and then OBE above the city.

In REM sleep you lose muscle tone, and therefore if the sleeper falls asleep in a position which is not supportive the sleep will experience the hypnogogic jerk. This sudden jerk quickly brings the awareness back which would have been useful for our ancestors to stop them falling off trees if they were to lose their balance whilst asleep.

In occultism this jerk is related to the astral body being pulled back into the physical body.

80. Learning to be psychic in a dream

MARCH 07, 2017

Another teaching dream featured being taught how to be psychic:

I was being taught how to have psychic ability I was with a group of people and we're in a class were all practicing on each other.

Some people are very good, some people were not but we're all learning and practicing together.

Next thing I knew I have to follow an old friend, so I saw an old friend and its transitioned to me being with my boyfriend and I were driving to another city.

This dream was odd as I could remember all of it, the teachings in the class and the outcomes I was able to achieve from the techniques taught.

81. Different Perspectives: Shared Dream

March 14, 2017

Shared dreams will often have different perspectives to the dreamers, whilst being the same dream:

I was with my ex-boyfriend walking into a clothes shop. I was looking at tops. Then for some reason I ask him to kiss me and he would not. For some reason I was begging him to kiss me, he said he would not kiss me.

A bit later for some reason I am hurting and devastated. We are travelling back to the car park and someone joined us I was trying to work out whether I must pay. I have lots of cash which I do not know where it has come from.

My ex-boyfriend is trying to calm someone down in the back and I am trying to drive to a police station.

My friend confirmed they had a dream in which they were shopping with my ex, their partner and myself when some bad people came. As part of a competition my ex and I won lots of cash, but my friend's partner was killed by these people.

My friend got in the car with us so we could take my friend to the police station.

82. Blue Alien Amphibious Beings

MARCH 15, 2017

The most odd lifeforms can appear in our dreams unlike anything we have seen in movies:

I was renovating a caravan that I had bought for cheap. I left the caravan and went to yoga.

When I came back to the caravan, I went to start ripping out the bathroom and I came across all these weird items.

One was an amazing watch by FUJI which could connect to something. This watch had amazing functionality, but it was no use to me because I could not use it as it was for someone's job role. It was steel color in gold and looked beautiful.

There was a certificate from this guy's work saying that he had personal responsibility for testing stocks and shares and there was a picture of him and his daughter. He had a very straight nose with dark hair she had very blonde hair.

In the bathroom there was a pull-down object to make the bathroom look like a mosaic wall but when you pulled it out a bath and toilet was revealed.

When I kept going outside there were all these amphibious beings and frog like things that were bright blue.

They were beings that humans now hunt.

This was one of the oddest dreams I had partly for the odd extreme details of the objects in the caravan and secondly due to the amphibious beings.

There was a knowing that these peaceful amphibious beings were hunted by people and they were just the most pleasant beings.

The technology of the watch in the dream was incredible and beyond anything we know today. What made the device interesting was the fact that it was in an average day looking watch container but the functionality was advanced.

83. Being a Spiritual Teacher

MARCH 15, 2017

Oddly, we can also be teachers ourselves within our dreams:

> *I was in a dream where I was a spiritual teacher that was living in a dome, in this dome I was teaching people how to meditate, relax their minds and how to do spiritual development*

I woke up to this memory feeling very real. I could remember at the time everything I had been teaching and the seriousness at which I taught it.

84. Taught How to be Psychic

APRIL 02, 2017

Often, we can have more than one teacher in a dream teaching us ESP abilities:

I was supposed to pick my friend up, but I went to the wrong place. During this time, I came across a party and around the corner was a setup of a house open to the public.

I sat in my car and a woman then started to talk to me, so I got out and I was talking to her. She taught me how to be psychic with information on how to see colors, how to close your eyes, etc.

She was testing my ability and asking me questions such as "Close your eyes then tell me what color comes to your brain.". I informed her I could see pink. She replied stating that color changing is good because it means that I was becoming physic.

Then her husband came, and he was trying to teach me how to be so psychic too. I stated that they were both interesting and I would love to carry on speaking to them. However, I needed to go and pick my mate up because I was running late so they let me go.

---

85. My Male Anima

APRIL 08, 2017

Sometimes I believe we can encounter ourselves in our dreams, Carl Jung would refer this as being my male anima, my masculine side:

I walked past a group of people when this stranger started to speak to me. As I am walking down the street, we are discussing my job as we happened to be going to the same place.

At this point we are deep in conversation and we enter a shop, he picks up an item he wanted then started to walk out the shop, but he had not paid.

This lady started to shout he grabbed me and took me down the stairs, but it felt like we floated.

The lady caught up with us, however, we disappear. I can see the lady searching for us, but she cannot see us, it is like we are in another dimension, but I feel I am this guy. It was a strange feeling.

The ability to just disappear from this ladies' view and take me to another dimension suggests the male dream character had control over my own dream. Hence, the possibility of this being another form of myself.

86. Nuclear Bomb

APRIL 15, 2017

There are often times when we do not see anything in a dream but instead can just feel something:

> *Suddenly there was a massive bang with an instantaneous blow out as if I had died from the force. It felt like a world war nuclear explosion.*
>
> *I could feel the force in my body and the push everything was black.*

When I awoke from this instant blast, I felt extremely worried. The feeling of instant death lingered with me and was extremely eerie.

I would definitely say this felt like a world war nuclear bomb. Over the coming days I was very alert of the news, however, thankful no war took place.

87. Conscious Astral Projection At Will

APRIL 17, 2017

One night I was trying to astral project all day long, hence by the time I went to bed I was absolutely shattered but kept telling repeating to myself, "Mind awake, body asleep".

I was intensively focusing my consciousness from the front of my head to behind my head. Suddenly, I could hear a swishing white noise sound followed by a very high pitch.

I could hear and feel my heart beating faster and faster followed by a very heavy feeling in my body, followed by a lifting sensation then back to a sinking sensation, alternating between these sensations constantly.

A person started to appear in my vision saying my name. This person was blonde and blue eyed, there was a feeling that he was an angel. There were beautiful pastel colors all around him, surrounding him as if it were an energy field or aura.

Illustration 13 The Angel Shows the angel I saw appearing in front of me, in the drawing I have added chakras as energy points on the

angel's body. The angel did not have wings when he appeared to me. However, due to the beautiful pastel colors surrounding him, I have drawn magnetic energy fields either side and above and below corresponding to the human energy field.

At this point I felt my consciousness lifting out of my physical body.

Suddenly, shouting, and loud noise from the physical world brought me out of the state. My neighbors were having a party and the screaming they were undertaking caused me to lose my state of control.

I was not impressed after all the effort I had put into the experience.

88. The Voice

APRIL 25, 2017

Dreams can feel as real as the waking life and provide interesting experiences:

> There was a voice coming from the wall of my flat and I was trying to discover where the voice was coming from.
>
> But it was in another dimension so I couldn't find it, but I could hear it. I was trying to figure out how to get at the voice, but I could not.

This dream was interesting as the person speaking has crossed between dimensions. Given the dream I had about **solving an equation** to exist in more than one dimension at once I wonder is this was showing the possibility to achieve simultaneous existence across dimensions.

89. Enjoying the Scene of the Astral Realm

APRIL 27, 2017

In our dreams we can sometimes appreciate the beautiful scenes we witness whilst dreaming:

I was in a field and the grass was a beautiful shiny green color with perfect blue clear sky.

There were beautiful sun rays shining down on me. I could feel the heat and warmth and decided to just enjoying walking through.

When dreams appear to provide us with such beauty and peacefulness, we can sometimes just take the enjoyment from them. These dreams often leave us waking up with a sense of calm and feeling of being refreshed.

Often these dreams can trigger us becoming conscious, however, because at the time we enjoy the dream we will just accept the scene.

90. The Huge Lucid Dream Mansion

APRIL 29, 2017

The buildings we can create in our dreams can be beautiful when we are fully conscious. Our lucidity allows us to control the aspects in our dreams to position the interiors exactly as we want:

I was in a dream walking down a street with my co-worker when I realize I was dreaming. I turned to my co-worker and willed him away. I wanted a famous person to appear instead but they did not.

Upset I walked towards my house and opened the door. I did not like the smallness of the house. As a result I decided to consciously change the size of the house as I knew I was dreaming. I pushed my hands out to make the corridor longer and put marble pillars either side of the corridor all the way along.

Next, I created some rooms including one with a Jacuzzi, a massive library room, cinema room, etc.

I sat in the library for a while reading but then I thought this was a bit of a waste for a lucid dream.

Then I made some friends appear to hang out with them. We all went outside on the balcony drinking.

Next thing an unknown man runs up to

*me and stabs with a knife. I woke up in
bed immediately with my heart pounding.*

Illustration 14 The Lucid Dream *Shows the pillars that were inserted by myself during my lucid dream to make the corridor appear grand and a roman era style.*

I was not happy that the dream finished so fast, however, I have noticed that when I have a lucid dream to maintain the consciousness this will happen. As my lucidity beings to winder I always find a traumatic event happening that pulls me out of the state and physically results in me waking up in bed.

This always happens with a sudden jolt and shock.

I recommend you look out for what your trigger is and learn to recognize it is your subconscious telling you it is time to wake up.

91. The Sharman Necklace

JUNE 22, 2017

In our dreams we can sometimes encounter the most interesting and mysterious objects:

I was walking down a street and stopped in front of a crystal shop. Suddenly, I find myself working for a millionaire in a massive mansion.

Confused by this jump I thought to transport myself back to the crystal shop. A friend of mine was now by my side, we walked into the shop.

Inside the crystal shop right in front of me was necklace with a thick rectangle crystal dangling off the chain. This necklace belonged to a Sharman. Amazed by the beauty of this necklace I brought it and put it on instantly.

Upon walking outside an authority figure stopped me and told me that I was not allowed to wear the crystal. The necklace was taken off me, I was annoyed.

Perhaps this object was an object in the astral realm that did not want to be moved hence why I was stopped. However, it is always important to note objects we see as we should be on the lookout for what they represent or finding the object in waking life.

92. Start of an OBE

JULY 01, 2017

One day I undertook a meditation session where I set the intent to astral project. Suddenly, there was a switch of my consciousness, 24 inches to my left, twice.

During the switch I realized I was out of my physical body and in the astral body, but my heartbeat was becoming louder and louder. An intense bright shining light shown through my window.

Suddenly there was a silence.

At this point I found myself in an unknown house with neighbors and family outside. I decide to go for a walk with my friend.

My friend and I are marveling at the beauty of the stars which appear intensively beautiful in the sky.

The pavement starts to turn into lava, we panic and start to run back to the house as fast as we can. We are a ten-minute run away. Running through the streets we are ducking and diving different pavement cracks.

I awake back in my room where I was meditating. Surprised I go downstairs and see that my door is open with the keys left in. I lock the door confused as to why the door was unlocked. Walking up the stairs I sense a presence, I turn around to check and see a guy at the door who looks like he has been in a fight.

I take him to the kitchen to clean his wounds. However, whilst in the kitchen my conscious self can see that he is holding a knife behind his back. He stabs me and I instantly awake from the meditation session.

During this session I was fully conscious, the dream was vivid. The guy that stabbed me shocked me into the physical reality from my meditation. Hence, I think the stab from dream character was a way for my subconscious mind to stop me falling into a dream, to remember the OBE and dream experience.

93. An Amazing Crystal House

I have seen the most amazing objects in my dreams and in this dream, I saw a house made of crystal:

I was standing in front of a huge crystal house, it was amazing, a geode crystal.

A lady bumped into me, I started to chat to her, and she told me this was her house. I told her how beautiful it was, and she invited me inside to look.

Inside were all these clear quartz crystals which were all shining.

Eventually, I walked through the house and carried on to where I was heading.

The house was unlike anything I had ever seen, the crystals were glowing and the energy was so intense and electrifying in a positive way with the utter most peace following through.

94. Bi Location

AUGUST 2017

He who thinks he knows everything is a fool. I live by this so always welcome the opportunity to speak to people on a subject I know well to find out more information and to catch anything I might have missed in my arrogance.

As such I decided to undertake a course in astral projection to develop my skills in August 2017 (27th).

This was my first attendance for a spiritual event, the workshop was on Consciousness and it was brilliant, reinforcing everything I knew or suspected.

Part of the workshop involved trying to project ourselves out of our body. The technique was the same technique I already knew and had been practicing since I was 7 years old that my father taught me. However, this time the difference is I was aware of people around me whilst undertaking the meditation.

There was around 20 of us in the room all laid next to each other on a blown-up bed. If one person moved, you would hear it.

After a period of time I began entering into the Hypnagogic state as usual, I continued to fight to stay with it, images were appearing including a beautiful sunset. I tried to stay with the images as much as possible.

I felt like I was in my home city in front of a rounded building. I stayed with this image and then was transferred to another planet with more than one moon and a rounded building on a tall tower.

Floating up in front of this tower I looked inside the tower trying to focus on what was inside, I could see a typewriter inside.

During this time, I was still aware of my physical

body lying on the blown-up bed surrounded by 20 people hearing the breathing of the people around me from the workshop in the physical whilst also being located on this other planet.

Illustration 15 Bi Location Planet *Shows the planet seen in the bilocation experience. The two moons are high up in the sky and a movable tower is seen in front of me which moved up and down on the pole. The tower building had windows all around.*

I focused back to the planet and the tower. I tried to gain better lucidly and leave the physical totally behind. I tried to achieve this by making the tower move up and down faster and faster on the pole it was held up on. I really tried to focus on the tower.

I could feel the movement of the tower, feeling myself on this planet, whilst at the same time I was feeling being in the room surrounded by people.

Annoyance was beginning to overcome my feelings, as I could feel my consciousness increasing more back to my physical body.

Eventually I my consciousness was fully back in the room. The instructor asked us what we each had experienced. Upon describing my experience, the instructor confirmed I had experienced bilocation. The ability to be in two places at once with your consciousness.

Another experience would happen in 2019, see The Doppelgangers.

95. The Incredible Mind of the Future

SEPTEMBER 17, 2017

This dream is one of my most incredible experiences and the reason why I wrote this book. It changed my life and gave me hope that our race does prosper and develop.

What I saw started from a meditation, as such I have not put this in dream quotes as technically, I was not dreaming as I had not gone to sleep.

I was meditating, ready to drift off to sleep when I hit the hypnagogic state. I suddenly became aware that I was walking down a spaceship corridor but as someone else, a lady with a dark-haired bob wearing a silver or metallic suit. I was in a space program, my mind was enhanced, I was super fit and healthy.

Upon realizing this I suddenly became aware of this incredible knowledge inside this "new brain". I was aware of mechanical engineering, the cosmic universe and advanced mathematics, I knew how the spaceship had been created and the knowledge of everything, the knowledge I had was just incredible.

I told about the Earth and humans and as fast as I could start to think about Earth, I saw in an instant the whole history of the Earth and the human race. Everything instantaneously flashed through my mind on the human race. It was as if I knew everything about the Earth and all living things on it. This knowledge was known as if it were ancient knowledge just like we would read about the Ancient Mayans, a lost ancient race.

Whilst this knowledge was in my head, I was at the same time seeing the Earth as if it were in my mind's eye. It was overwhelming the amount of knowledge I had in a split of a second.

I decided to think about something else and

looked in front of me as I looked at the corridor, I instantly knew how it was constructed, the complicated mathematical equations that had come together to create the structure that I was in flying through interstellar space. If you had asked me to reconstruct this craft, I would be able to and draw out all the mathematical equations needed and structural drawings. The intelligence was another level unexplainable.

Illustration 16 I Saw the Future *Shows the corridor seen in the meditation experience with the lady that I became aware I was. The planet represents what I saw in her mind as I was experiencing the whole history of the Earth and mankind within a split of a second whilst also seeing the Earth in my mind's eye.*

I suddenly came back to reality, I felt like a chimp in comparison to how intelligent this lady was and it made me wonder if in thousands of years' time will the human race think as I experienced and if so they will think we were very simple minded.

I went to bed and had a dream:

I went to an inventor building and asked my purpose in life. I was told I was going to invent something important.

I wish that someone was able to read my mind as I was having this experience. In 2005 scientists showed evidence that visual areas in the brain contain information to predict perception (Kamitani & Tong, 2005).

In further studies scientists have been able to record dream visuals to record dreams their participants were having (Horikawa, et al., 2013). They were able to categorize the dream contents as the visuals showed dream activity to be the same as waking life (Stromberg, 2013). These scientists were able to predict dreams with a 75% accuracy.

It would be amazing if these scientists could have studied my brain and seen what I saw. Or perhaps my brain would have blown the machine up due to the speed of which this information can into my brain.

96. A Future Time Traveler

AUGUST 05, 2017

In my mind's eye I can still see everything from this dream and the feelings nearly three years later:

I was a time traveler with the ability to go forward or back in time. The device that only I used to achieve this travel was kept behind a vaulted door.

One day I decided to travel twenty years into the future. Upon travelling into the future, I fell in love with a guy.

One day I went back to the location of my time travel device and turned the vault, I continued to travel but kept returning to the love of my life.

One day my love's uncle told me that he knew what I was doing, and he was also a time traveler, as he had the same alchemist ability to achieve time travel.

He said I needed to stop travelling as if I was in love with his nephew, he couldn't afford me getting stuck in the past. I took the decision to travel no more and stay with my love in the future.

---

97. The Prayer Beads

SEP/OCT 2017

I had a dream about a certain formula, when I googled the formula that I dreamt about the results equaled 109. I then searched for this number which led to prayer beads.

I decided to order some, however, upon arrival they broke on first use.

Having had a dream that led me to purchase an item which then breaks upon being used, which they were not supposed to, led me to wonder if this was just my subconscious testing me to see if I was listening to my dreams.

98. A Shape Shifter

SEPTEMBER 10, 2017

Carl Jung talks about different archetypes in our dreams and the meanings behind each of these in his books. One of these archetypes is the shape shifter which I encountered in one of my dreams:

A guy broke into my tree house, I told him I was going to kill him, but he got to me first and killed me.

He morphed into my mum before I had arrived somewhere, and all this stuff was in my tree house and I was embarrassed as it looked a state. There was coldness coming from an open window.

I went to turn the lights off as I saw the guy entering.

The shapeshifter character in a dream is able to become anything at will in the dreams often to deceive the dreamer. However, in this dream it was interesting that I was able to spot the shapeshifter in the dream.

A theory I hold is that Baphomet is a shapeshifter, he can become any shape at will to bring fear to the dreamer but if you face him he loses all his power.

99. The Hypnagogic State

SEPTEMBER 12, 2017

When your dream recall grows strong you will notice more interesting dreams all within the same night.

Not only this but before you go to sleep you will start to become more conscious of the fact that you are falling asleep and able to grab hold of the hypnagogic stage. The hypnagogic state is a bizarre state between both waking and sleeping. If you can catch this stage, then you can potentially go straight into a lucid dream or an out of body experience.

I decided to try to achieve the hypnagogic state by thinking about the black that I could see as I closed my eyes, laid on the bed. After a while I started to see images which turned into a medieval castle.

I was in a room with bars, a jail. I could feel people behind me. I was a person sat in this jail.

During this visualization I was telling myself to stay with the thoughts however, eventually I drifted off.

This is why it is important to control the mind, the stronger the grasp on our minds wandering the more we are able to control the travelling of our consciousness.

Hence, why monks will meditate to control their consciousness with the ultimate aim to be conscious for the whole day even whilst their bodies sleep.

100. Taught Thought Form to Create Objects

SEPTEMBER 15, 2017

Characters in our dreams appear to help us understand the dream world and how to program various aspects to react how we want:

I was in my penthouse apartment that had an open roof overlooking the city. I went into my front room and saw my neighbor's cat, but I knew it was not her. A voice came in to tell me that this the cat was created from my thought forms.

"What you are doing now is your using thought forms to create an image of kitty, but it is not kitty." I was being taught how to create a version of the neighbor's cat "kitty" using thought form, she was near real but red. I was stroking her then she started to get aggressive, so I started to run away.

I didn't trust the cat or the guy. A voice said, "You should trust me I am your tutor, I am trying to teach you!". I replied, "Ok I am sorry", but it was too late, I woke up.

The fact that in our dreams we can consciously create beings from thought forms alone is incredible. However, there seems to still be glitches when trying to replicate beings as seen in this situation.

I wonder who the tutor was, my higher self or a spirit guide. Often these people that are guiding me or teaching me in my dream have different voices.

101. The Trickster Encounter

SEPTEMBER 19, 2017

Certain characters in our dreams can have different meanings and try to teach us different things. These different characters in dream analysis are know as archetypes. This dream demonstrates that of the Trickster archetype:

I was aiming to travel out of the city. Upon walking along a road and I came across a person that I started to walk with.

This person kept insisting we go one direction, then suddenly changing to another direction.

I suddenly felt this person was untrustworthy and leading me off the right path and into the wrong path.

Upon realizing this the Trickster exposed itself through jumping into the pavement to change shape. I fought against her and found the right path.

Upon travelling out of the city I could see a mass of evil vehicles travelling towards where I had been with the Trickster.

The trickster archetype represents hidden advice, showing where your vulnerabilities are in life. This dream was symbolic of this showing me that I was being led down a dangerous path.

It is important to monitor our dreams and look out

for key characters as they can provide great insight into ourselves and life. I recommend you keep a reflective log on different characters so that when they appear you know exactly what they represent.

When you encounter one of the archetypes the dream is more intense, and this character will stick out from normal characters. They will be unlike your usual suspects. That is if you commonly dream about a certain person, their behavior in dreams becomes predicable, this is not the case with an archetype character, you will be surprised by their presence.

Carl Jung was a psychologist that supported the theory of insight into mental health through the analysis of dreams. Jung believed dream symbols provided insight into the dreamer's mental health and could potentially help with treatment of issues.

These dream signs appear to come from the human collective unconscious and carry meaning about the dreamers' emotional. Scientist in recent studies (Bradshaw & Storm, 2012) found dream analysis could be explored for clinical use.

Whilst in NYC, USA on a trip I discovered the Carl Jung Institute in Manhattan, the amount of books that were located there were incredible and they undertake a huge number of development programs on the Jung dream analysis.

102. The Egyptian Amulet

SEPTEMBER 24, 2017

Dreams can often point us into areas of research:

My father gave me a book on astrology as he wanted my opinion on it.

I told him the symbols were not planet symbols and did not make sense. They were some type of symbols. However, I was able to read these symbols.

In the book I saw a arm bracelet with a sun at the top and beads around and long things at the bottom. There was instructions on how to create this bracelet in the book.

Upon waking I drew the bracelet I saw.

Illustration 17 Egyptian Amulet *Shows the amulet that I saw in my dream. A round shape at the top followed by different beads throughout the bracelet and finished with longer beads in a different shape*

on the bottom. All the beads were different colors. I do not remember the colors.

When I googled this bracelet, I found it was an amulet from the ancient Egyptian age, known as a *pectoral.*

I did search for the astrology book cover I remembered seeing from the dream of which I found. Upon reading this book talked about using karma and astrology to transform your soul.

103. Discussing a Curse: Elixir

NOVEMBER 24, 2017

In our dreams we can often meet characters that try to alert us to a problem in our lives:

> *I was supposed to meet someone, but that person let me down. People were fighting with outsiders. I was with mum and my work colleagues.*
>
> *A lady was there, she had tarot cards and was stating that she was surprised I was not more successful. I then proceeded to tell her about a curse that was put on me and that it was part of the reason why I was not as successful. She said I needed to drink some elixir.*
>
> *My mum and I went outside to get a taxi.*

This dream was odd due to the tarot reader and the advice. Upon reviewing this dream, I searched for the term elixir, as I did not understand what elixir was.

My findings showed elixir is believed to be associated with Alchemy and the philosophers stone. Perhaps the lady in the dream was telling me to clean my energy field and elixir was reference to the energy of the world.

104. Viewing a Friends Dream

MAY 09, 2018

Now after the **demon encounter dreams** I stopped sharing dreams with my friend. However, one night I had a dream out of the ordinary which I was not a participate in:

I remember seeing some type of alien being. The dream was in the third person form.

The being was hiding in a cave and dragging people in eating them into its stomach.

Due to the nature of the dream I asked my friend about their dream to which they confirmed they had dreamt about a demon beast killing people and just remembered stone walls.

105. The Squatters a Shared Dream

JULY 30, 2018

I mentioned to some work colleagues I could sometimes enter into others dreams that night:

I was living in a massive house when people started to come in to live in the house. They were homeless people and wanted to live in the house.

I was trying to organize them as there were so many people. I was giving them different roles such as security, chef, etc. My friend came and I was asking her advice on how to get rid of them as she had the same problem.

My friend has never appeared in any of my dreams at this point, so I thought it odd for their appearance. As such I contacted her and asked if she had dreamt about homeless people. She proceeded to say not homeless people but squatters in a building.

I found this too much of a coincidence and I am pretty certain a homeless person is also technically a squatter it's just our different perspectives.

The same week I then had another experience with one of the colleagues from the group that asked me to enter their dreams.

I was walking towards an interview room with my colleague. We were called in by the interviewer.

The interviewer was interviewing my colleague.

All of a sudden, we are running away from the room, down the corridor. I lose my colleague and search for a hiding place.

The next morning, I asked my colleague to write his dream down. We swapped notes. He had reported that I was with him for an interview of which suddenly the lady turned into a monster and we had to run away. He said he was looking for me but couldn't find me.

Then another I shared another dream with a third colleague from the same group:

I was walking down the street and I see my colleague driving towards me with a lady sat in the passenger seat of the white van he is driving.

I ask for a lift to a few streets over, they agree, and I thank them and tell them to enjoy the rest of their night.

This colleague said he could not remember his dram. As such I said what I had dreamt. He was very embarrassed when I told him of the dream as he said he had met a lady for a date in the first time in months that night and had picked her up in his van but did not want to tell anyone about it.

The interesting thing is after I was able to enter into everyone's dream the once I did not enter into any more of their dreams.

106. The Doppelgangers

NOVEMBER 05, 2019

One night I had a dream where I was with my partner travelling in my father's city. Upon awakening my partner reported a similar dream with me present.

Now what is interesting is my father phoned me angry that I had not told him I was visiting his city. I was confused and asked him what he meant as I live on the other side of the world and would have been sleeping when he reported seeing my partner and myself.

He reported that he seen both of us walking along a road. He described our clothes and my favorite boots which he has never seen. What made this weirder was the exact time he reported seeing us was the exact time my heart dropped to its lowest point of 43bpm. I do not know what my father saw all I do know is the time he reported seeing us lined up with the time we were sleeping, and we did dream about being in that location.

Perhaps this was our astral forms travelling, the doppelgangers of people have been reported as being seen by others throughout history. There are numerous cases where someone's double has appeared to others. A few cases I have read featured a doctor who would be reported walking through the streets of London ignoring those around him however, he was unaware of this and physically in his office.

Another case featured a schoolteacher whose doppelganger would appear somewhere else whilst she was teaching, this would freak out the school children and she would have to keep changing jobs.

When people see another's doppelganger, they have reported not being able to interact with them.

107. Other lives

One thing is for sure, the following dreams are different to my others. I cannot work out whether they are glimpses into parallel universes or past or future lives. As such I have called these experiences out separately from my other dreams.

I do believe in reincarnation. As I state elsewhere in this book, that which you hate you will become if your horrible to a set of people you will more than likely be both into that group. This is why you must not try to judge.

Likewise, those that inflict suffering and pain will be born into a life in which they suffer as they inflicted. Do not think people get away with things for they will be judged, their own soul will judge them. I believe this is why people turn to alcohol and drugs to block out feelings they cannot cope with this does not solve the problem.

I also believe we can witness our past and future lives due to time not being linear in other dimensions. Therefore, through tapping into the dream world you are able to cross time, and this leads to experiencing other lives or perhaps other universes.

108. The Farmer's Kid

FEBURARY 27, 2016

This was an odd dream as I felt like I was the young girl, and this was my life:

I was a young girl around six to seven years in age. I lived on a farm with my family including my Mother, Father, three brothers, a sister, and an uncle.

A psycho killer came in one day and started killing everyone.

Dad hid me in the house so the psycho killer wouldn't kill me. The house was made of wood and there were hidden corridors which is where I was hidden.

Psycho killer came up to my Dad and uncle in kitchen as they were sat at the table waiting for him. As he approached them Dad made an action for me to shoot the Psycho killer.

I shot the Psycho killer.

This dream was very traumatic in that all my family got massacred expect my father and uncle. The Psycho killer was evil. The people in my dream were not my family in the physical life, I did not recognize them, however, I did feel that this was my life.

109. Special Forces

MARCH 14, 2016

The following was a dream where I was an undercover military guy:

I am an undercover man working in a special forces section with big muscles listening to a woman briefing me and another guy about our mission we are about to undertake.

We jump over a high wall with barbed wires across it. We go through all the barriers and get to a group of people.

We are in the enemies clothing as such we cannot be recognized and blend in with the enemy well.

The women that gave us the briefing goes off to do something she needed to do. The guy and I are left there waiting when everyone is gathered into the room, we happen to be in.

The commander says someone has broken in and they are pretending to be us. I stay calm listening to him.

The group commander is finding it hard to find us. Then a lady appears and says all the men should get naked as will remember each other's bodies.

> *At this point I start to panic as I have a 10.5-inch penis and I will stand out from the other guys.*
>
> *It all kicks off and I get my gun out and a gun battle kicks off. I wake up.*

I found this such a funny dream it was hilarious to recall. I feel this was a past life, perhaps one of the most recent. Another similar experience would happen a month later, April 11, 2016, where the same military guy would appear in my dream:

> *I was a guy away on a military exercise sat on a hill which was a mountain, looking down over terrain overlooking all the territory.*
>
> *I was sat there with a small fire celebrating something such as a completed mission.*
>
> *I was so proud of myself and felt like the mission had been a huge accomplishment for me. I was sat with a very small bottle of wine in celebration.*

I believe this was my most recent past life. Interestingly I spoke to a retired friend who was in the marines in the 1960s and states they would take a small bottle which they would then drink to celebrate when completing a mission.

Illustration 18 Special Services Mission *Shows the solider that I was sitting up high looking down on terrain below. He is up on a hill with a very small fire. There are mountains all around.*

I always wanted to join the military however could not sure to be a migraine sufferer, which stopped me from entry into the army. People do comment that my nature would be well suited to the military.

Sometimes we will be born with certain aspects to stop us from undertaking the same type of life again. For this reason, I believe I was born a migraine suffered to stop me from going into the military as I have had too many past lives over the last 2000-3000 years in the military.

110. The Smart Female

JULY 22, 2016

Another dream I had that I believe is a future life:

I was an incredibly smart African female that was not living in Africa however, I was on my way back to Africa to see my father who lived there.

When I arrived, I discovered that my father's business colleagues were trying to con him out of his money.

He instructed me to blow his business up, he told me exactly how and where to do it. I did not want to, but he insisted it was the only way forward. I did it.

I believe this dream was one of my past or future lives as I felt I knew this girl and I was this girl. My soul felt the same as hers, In the dream I knew the location incredibly well.

Timewise I cannot date the dream as I did not recall the technology around, this is why I assume this is a future life due to the ability to get hold of equipment to blow up my fathers' business for him with ease, and the fact we are now a more global community where we can travel to other countries to work in.

The education I had felt more advanced that my current education in my current life, as this girl was extremely smart and had access to technology, hence, why I feel this may have been a future life.

111. The Military Camp

OCTOBER 01, 2016

Another military dream that felt real:

I was a male in a military camp, I was getting ready for the evening having had a shower chatting to my fellow soldiers in my quarters when the sergeant suddenly appeared.

We all had our private parts visible as we as we were not fully dressed, and all looked scruffy. We had not had time to make our quarters.

The sergeant said, "Right you got a minute to get decent and sort all this crap out". We all crazily tried to tidy everything up as fast as we could. Trying to make our quarters whilst getting dressed.

As the Sergeant came back into the quarters I was struggling to zip up on my bottoms, this movement must have caught his eye as he shouted at me to stop moving. I was terrified.

This dream I believe was a future or past life. I was not sure the country nor the timeline as the focus was only on the quarters. A future or past life will reappear in our dreams with different scenes. An example of this includes the following dream a month later in in December where I would find myself in an armored tank in another military style dream:

I am in an armored tank which keeps being shot at. I am frantically trying to fix the walls of the tank to stay alive.

Perhaps the dreams are related to other military dreams in that they are the same character or life.

I never have reoccurring dreams, unlike my grandfather who reports the same dream every single night! Therefore, it is very unusual that I dream about being in the military so vividly. This would make sense if this were my most recent past life.

If you happen to start noticing the same type of life in your dream not related to your current life, I would indeed recommend you start to track these dreams. Search for patterns and similarity. Start to explore if these were indeed past lives.

112. Fluency in another Language

FEBUARY 13, 2016

Sometimes dream can be freaky due to their unexplainable detailed nature on other people's lives:

I was fighting with someone under a swimming pool where there were trap doors everywhere.

The bad guy I was fighting I manage to chuck into the pool with crocodiles, but he got out. I trapped him in a trap door with snakes and spiders and then flooded everything.

All of a sudden, I become this girl and I am with the owner of the pool and the family. We have to do whatever he says.

He started to argue with people as he wanted to drain the water. I stuck up for his brother and he was not happy and tried to strangle me.

The guy took me back to my house (the girl's house). I knew it was my house as there was a picture of myself (this girl) as a 7-year-old. He started to strangle me, and his brother took a video of me. However, they spoke a different language so I must not have been English.

The brother called another guy to say come over referring to me being a 17-year-old. I tried to fight back and tried to

> *strangle him.*
>
> *This older guy turned up in a 4x4 whilst this was happening.*
>
> *Next, I go from being this girl to a third perspective watching this girl being carried out into the 4x4 by these guys.*

The details of this dream were intense, I could speak the other language fluently in my dream however I did not know what language it was when I woke up.

Illustration 19 The Room *The side cabinet I saw with a picture frame on of the girl in the room she was attacked.*

Another aspect which was interesting was the fact my perspectives shifted after they had killed the girl, from being a first-person perspective to a third person perspective.

113. 40 Years as a Male

FEBURARY 27, 2016

This dream was the longest dream I have ever remembered in my life, the duration was actually longer than my life at the time. This dream lasted for forty years:

I was a guy for 40 years. I experienced him growing up, meeting his wife, his accountancy job from 9am to 5pm every day during the week, and other life events.

I remember experiencing the emotions of crying with job at the birth of his first daughter.

I experienced his daughters 21st birthday at which I was crying with pride.

I physically woke up from this dream thinking how the hell I have just lived a life longer than mine.

Due to the length of time span of this dream and the whole life experience I had, this dream confused me. This perhaps was a past life due to the emotions I felt that I had never been in an experience to feel. Or perhaps I was tapping into the collective unconscious of a guy living this life or a parallel life in another multi universe.

Interestingly I received a result of 92% in my accounting exam for my MBA.

114. A Man in the Medieval Days

OCTOBER 04, 2016

With the following dream I really felt like I was the man as if this was part of a life I had previously lived:

I was a man with a woman in the medieval days. I was being exiled from the town.

The woman was saying she was going to come with me and telling me how much she wanted to be with me. I agreed for her to come.

I was buff with a massive sword and extremely manly.

I believe this was a past life of mine, I felt intensely as if I were this man and recognized the situation. He had a lot of my characteristics.

Illustration 20 Medieval past-life *Shows the man I was walking along a path with a lady who loved him.*

The man reminded me a bit of the main character from the game Witcher.

115. The Love Story

OCTOBER 27, 2016

Our dreams can show us stories that can have a larger meaning behind them and almost be of a fable nature. The following shows a sad dream of mine:

I was on an island with three men, we were undertaking illegal activities. Law enforcers came and started to shoot us.

During this time, one of the guys on my team, came across a woman who he fell in love with. He asked for permission to marry her and they got married.

One day she suddenly died. He inherited all her money, but he did not want the money, he wanted her.

One day, years later, he met another women who he again married. However, she also died. He inherited more money.

Finally, he married a third women, the exact same thing happened. His friends stated how great it was he had inherited all this money. However, he did not want the money he wanted the company of the women he loved.

He ended up living a lonely unhappy life.

---

116. My Smart Daughter

NOVEMBER 14, 2016

Some dreams can feature us having children that we have never seen, of which we can be their mother or father in the dream:

I had a young daughter with blonde hair and blue eyes. She was such a sweet child and would do everything that I asked of her. She was incredibly smart.

I believe this was a future life due to two points. Firstly, in the dream I showed incredible love towards her.

Secondly, when you have a dream in the future the intelligence in people and technology that you encounter is different to today's world. You find it fascinating. The level of intelligence of this child was as if the kids in that age of history were taught at an extremely high level, different to this decade.

117. Past Life Regression

MARCH 2017

I was due to undergo an operation and as such if I died, I wanted to ensure that I had connected with any past lives before passing. Up to this point I had dreams which I thought were connected to past lives and had feelings about my past lives however I was not entirely convinced whether it was just in my mind.

My father had taught me to self-hypnotize and during the years I had attempted to connect with my past lives. This connection had shown me to be a roman military commander and various other roles with a lot focused on military activity.

I had also performed various past life regressions on others with successful outcomes leading them to discover answers.

I wanted a 'professional' to send me under, I wanted to check if what I thought and had witnessed cross referenced. This would remove any doubts. As such I arranged for a professional hypnotist to hypnotize me.

The day of my hypnotism I had booked the afternoon off from work, however, I was very lucky as a massive crystal quartz I had ordered arrived that morning over a week earlier than scheduled. The crystal came in a box which I had to get colleagues to help me carry to the crystal to my car. As such the crystal would be travelling with me for the day.

Upon arriving at the location of the hypnotist I went and knocked on the office door. I went inside and she talked me through the process. From everything she described this was as per my normal self-hypnotism process only I would not be staying it I would simply be listening.

I laid back on the chair as she started to instruct my subconscious, this process was more relaxing as I was not in charge. As she was counting back my body started to feel as if it were floating and rocking back and forth in the chair. I remembered thinking wow this is a very sensitive chair.

The hypnotist instructed me to open a door to my past life. As I opened that door I looked down at my feet, they belonged to a man wearing sandals, this guy was walking through what appeared to be a camp in a field near a forest.

As I was walking kids were running past me and other people would smile and say hello to me. I was in a military camp where I was a general. There were many people that knew me as they were following my orders. I was leading thousands of people into battle.

The hypnotist skipped me forward to nearer my death, I was in my tent and some people burst in from the enemy side. I tried to fight them off, but they murdered me. I was dead. The hypnotist took me to the spiritual world to discover why I had been taken at the height of my leadership before reaching glory. It turned out I had been murdered at that point as had I been successful then I would have killed to many of the enemy and the spiritual world did not want that to happen. I gave acceptance and left the door closing it behind me.

Next the hypnotist took me back further into one of my earlier past lives. I was a female with curly blonde hair and blue eyes, I was extremely pretty, too pretty. One day in a field with a male friend we were both attacked, and I was raped and murdered. This trauma in my spirit would linger and result in me having fewer lives as a female to be more focused on reincarnations as a male. I found this interesting for as a young girl I always had a fascination with curly hair and longed to have curly blonde hair.

When I was brought out of the hypnotism, I mentioned how comfortable the chair was as it made me rock intensively. However, hypnotist confirmed I had not physically been rocking in the chair and the chair I discovered could not rock as I had felt it do so.

This freaked me out as I had physically felt this rocking, my astral body must have been what I had been feeling and not the physical self.

The hypnotist told me to try to get some clear quartz crystal for protection, when I responded I had a massive clear quartz crystal in my car in a box she was shocked. Especially when I mentioned the crystal was not due for another week. I believe this crystal came early for protection.

When you undergo energy or past life work such as this people recommend clear quartz crystal as it is supposed to protect your energy as these activities often drain your energy.

118. A Pause in My Dreams

In early 2018, I was ridiculed by someone that I knew for my dreams, they said my ability to remember my dreams was freaky and other hateful things. This affected me so much I stop recalling my dreams, choosing to ignore them.

I tried to bury this ability.

A few months later I felt "normal", I hid that aspect of myself, however, I was not happier. A few months later and I decided to throw myself into something to distract me from my dreams.

I started a part-time MBA whilst working full time. This through me out of my dreams and into study, full force. I would complete the MBA in 17-months during which time I would move flats four times, work full-time for 10 months, and move to another country.

I was awakened again in March 2020, during the COVID-19 crisis, nearly two years later, this led me to get interest again into my dreams and write this book.

Not soon after I had a really interesting dream featuring an entity that looked like a demon. When I looked this demon up it corresponded to a demon that the Knights Templar were aware of and thought symbolized awakening the minds of people that had seen it. This was very interesting.

When I started reading about the Knights Templar, I had this weird feeling that I was one in a past life and this is how I was able to have these weird spiritual experiences and out of body experiences at such a young age perhaps. As this was stuff that they reportedly would practice according to legends.

Spirituality is not always black and white. You can go into and out of being spiritual throughout periods in your life. I have known many people to be told they are too young or that felt they were too young in their thirties or forties and did not pick up being spiritual again until they retire. I understand this for life can become very busy, especially when starting a family.

Illustration 21 Baphomet *Shows the demon I saw in my dream with his huge horns. Wings were not seen on the demon in the dream however have been added in the drawing along with fire to represent awakening, symbolizing the demon is bringing light and awareness to see the reality of the world. The staff of Hermes Trismegistus known as the caduceus has been added to the other hand of the demon corresponding to kundalini energy rising through the different charkas as representing that the active engagement in kundalini will bring about the seeing of the reality and truth as the staff in mythology wakes the sleeping. The demon has a female body with a male head to represent androgyny which is the balancing of body sides a key aspect of alchemy. The demon is known as Baphomet which in Latin and read backwards means Sophia. Baphomet was supposedly a demon that the knight templars reported seeing in occult activities such as astral projection to symbolize enlightenment of seeing the truth was taking place. Hence, there is a cross representant of the symbol of the Knights Templar at the top of the door on the right-hand side. The words veritas vos liberabit in Latin translates to 'the truth will set you free', followed by veritas lux mea that truth is the light, hence why the demon has the light in his hand. I am shown as I am watching the demon with a knife ready to attack.*

Another case of people stepping away from spirituality is when they fear their experiences. I have known talented people, capable of things that I am not, that have switched their spirituality off as they have seen too much and do not want to see anything more any longer. Their experiences are so intense they are simply overwhelmed.

Now what I have shared with you in this book, simply a few years of my dreams from 2015 to 2017, can you imagine the hundreds or even possibly thousands of experiences I would have had if I had not told my subconscious to close that aspect of myself.

I know what I have saw, and I have seen things that most claim not to have ever seen. However, I believe everyone can turn these things on they just choose to block them out.

As an example, it happened to me. I went from five dreams a night, remembering every dream I had. To not remembering any because I chose to block them. I had started to see entities from my friend's dreams.

I decided to stop sharing dreams with my friend and I told my subconscious to block them out. Now what I have shared with you in this book, simply a few years of my dreams from 2015 to 2017, can you imagine the hundreds or even possibly thousands of experiences I would have had if I had not told my subconscious to close that aspect of myself.

If you have lived a life where you have committed crimes or hurt people, it is not too late to turn your life around. We are centenarians, meaning we are more likely than ever to live to 100 years of age now.

Imagine if soon we are able to reverse ageing than retirement will be a thing of the past, simply more people will just choose to have sabbaticals. The advances we will gain will become incredible as the experts will not have to retire due to old age and bad health.

Let us try to advance our society through trying to focus on gaining advancements for the benefit of humankind.

I believe our minds are the most beautiful things in the universe. Rather than seeking all these adrenaline activities why do we not seek to investigate the inner workings of the mind. Unlocking its potential.

Illustration 22 Always Trust Your Subconscious *Showing an androgynous individual of both male and female the key to balance the aim of alchemy. On the left top corner is the moon with the opposite symbol the sun at the top right. Likewise, the mountains are shown on one side with snow for the frozen water (ice) the opposite to the flowing lake with moving water. The symbol of a heart is shown in the center with rings showing that love will give you wings to lighten your soul. The pillars are to center the picture and the words "The Route We Think Is Wrong Is Right, Always Trust The Subconscious" is written with a 's' missing from the subconscious to symbolize the fact this word would be classified as spelt wrong. However, do you actually notice straight away, and if not then why is it wrong, if you are not aware of it. Likewise, we often think we are going down a wrong path but how do we know this is the wrong path as we do not know our own soul plans, perhaps we are being dealt karma from a past life.*

We should develop our souls and others souls aiming to instill joy into every individual we encounter. If if that joy is minimal. A small ripple can cause a huge effect in the world. We should always seek to understand both sides and acknowledge that we cannot always be right.

What the mind and the subconscious can give you is hard to put into words, but I guarantee you when you experience just a glimpse of something such as the Superconsciousness it will change your world forever. A new world will open up to you.

My aim in life is through this book to help people awaken, why? Because I want people to enhance their own minds, to become happy and beautiful beings. Imagine the possibilities if everyone of us could come up with some invention to change the world.

I, have seen, the future, and it is beautiful. I have seen thousands of years into the future and we will carry out interstellar travel. As I write this now with certainty, I am receiving goosebumps of energy through my whole body for I know it is certain.

Our minds will be enhanced with infinite knowledge that delivers information so fast to us, we will seem godlike compared to how we are today. If I could put that experience into you, like I did you would marvel at the incredibleness of our future minds and how we will think. Right now, I feel primitive compared to how I did feel in that experience.

This universe is a beautiful place and we should enjoy it and aim to break out of the confined prisons that we build for our minds.

Sometimes the reality is clear to see but yet we seem to ignore that reality and go with the myth instead. We take this myth for truth never seeking to see the real reality that lies in front of us or not seeking to explore and discover the truth for ourselves.

We should open our eyes to seek the truth for ourselves to know the reality compared to the myth. Myth can lead to false knowledge and hiding the true nature of the world.

Now I will start to end my book on a few points, firstly, a point I know everyone knows but yet we all ignore, even me at times.

Why do we focus so much energy on becoming wealthy and making money, when we know when we die our soul is all that is carried over?

Why do we not invest more time on developing ourselves, our morals, and our knowledge?

Illustration 23 The Peacock Egg *Showing myself meditating on my energy field known as the peacock egg in alchemy. I am seen with wings inside the egg, which have developed through the result of energy focused upon them to develop these wings. These wings lead to flying in the other dimension of the astral world. Six small eggs have been drawn, three below me and three above to represent as above, so below, an alchemical known term. However, three eggs are cracked below to show you cannot fly in the reality dimension as you can in the astral dimension. A peacock male is shown on the left of the picture and a female peacock on the right to show opposites with the corresponding symbols below them of male and female. A lock is on the left-hand side with the key on the right-hand side. The Moon is seen on the top left quarter and the Sun in the top right quarter to symbolize the difference between the day. One egg is shown with horns to represent bad and another with an angel halo to represent good.*

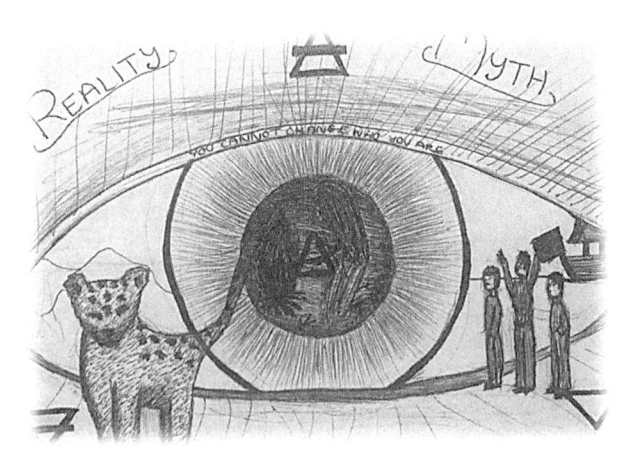

Illustration 24 See The Truth *Shows myself in the pupil of the eye, sitting by a fire with the alchemical symbol of fire in the middle. The alchemical symbol above the eye for air is seen with the symbol for Earth at the bottom left and water at the bottom right. On the left side of the picture is seen a young snow leopard cub with snow mountains behind and on the right three explorers having arrived at shore through travelling on a boat. The scene represents the three people creating a myth about a monster cat from their travels. However, in reality, the monster cat is simply a very young snow leopard cub. The overall eye represents seeing the whole truth as it is through understanding what is myth compared to reality. This is representant of the words you cannot change who you are as that is the truth.*

I believe that we are born again and again, with others being further or earlier in their reincarnation cycle that others.

I believe that if you hate on one type of person or group than you will be born into that group or born that type of person to appreciate the good in them and their point of view. Even if you cannot understand it. The trick is to accept people, everyone, within reason, for who they are.

If you do not like for example the opposite sex, then you will be born that opposite sex to feel the pain that you inflicted upon that person. Likewise, if you dislike a certain group of people you will then be born into living into that group of people to witness what you have inflicted.

Therefore, it is better you do not show dislike to others as you risk being born into a situation to receive that which you put out.

For this reason, I ensure not to hate on people.

Another aspect of what I believe happens in reincarnation is that the more you build up bonds with people or connections you will then have an easier life with them in your next life.

For example, if you meet someone at work and you clash. In your next life, if you come across them, you both unconsciously, will have a dislike toward each other. Therefore, it is better to try to build up a rapport with everyone you meet to ensure the encounters in your next live are positive.

This is why, I believe sometimes we meet people that we instantly connect with as we have built bonds with them in a past life.

For example, I constantly encounter people that just instantly dislike me and treat me very bad for no reason. I have even called people out on this and they have said they do not know why but they simply do not like me. I believe perhaps in a past life when I was a roman military commander they were on my enemy's side in a past life. Due to the size of an army I would have not known who they were. Therefore, I have no ill will towards them. However, they would have known who I were and would have had this ill will towards me.

I believe our energy field accumulates throughout our lives therefore the more we work on it the stronger is comes back throughout our lives. One example of this can be seen when I went into a store that sold crystals.

Upon entering I was greeted by a guy, initially I distrusted him however we did start to chat. After I built up trust with him, I asked him how my chakras looked. He stared around me, checking my energy field and started to sense my energy. He commented that my energy was stronger than his which he was not happy about. He stated he had been developing as a Sharman over the last 10 years and had rarely seen an energy field like mine. He said he could see wings, which he had never seen before.

This made me chuckle as I thought given my karma in life I have been dealt, perhaps I am more of a fallen angel. Casted down to Earth to try to do good for that I have done wrong in the past.

This comment had been echoed previously when I went to visit my father one day. Arriving in a social gathering place he introduced me to a friend, she said my father had told her everything about my experiences. She stated my energy was incredibly intense and being a Reiki Healer, she had only ever encountered this energy from her trainer.

Interestingly this person worked with murderers and criminals for their day job. I found something not right about her energy. Because of this feeling, I do not know why I did it, but I imagined a mirror in front of me to reflect any thoughts or energy back onto her, whether it was positive or negative.

A few minutes later she remarked that I had a defense up, I denied it and carried on talking to her. Then she spilled her drink on herself. She was annoyed said she did not know how but I was doing something to her.

At this point I commented that I did not have a problem with her, however, anything she felt against me would two-fold back on her. Hence if she were positive, she would receive that two-fold back and have a great evening. However, if she were to choose negatively then she would receive that thought form back. She got freaked out and suddenly she then fell off her chair. At this point she stopped being negative.

Unfortunately, a lot of people who undertake what they classify as spiritual work have not fully understood it. They state they believe in reincarnation but hate on a certain group of people or treat some people cruelly.

Why do I receive comments on my energy so much, I do not know. Perhaps, it is due to an accumulation of energy throughout my lives. Hence, why I was having OBEs at such a young age or perhaps it was spending four and a half years living alone in solitude developing this energy in my late twenties. Perhaps both.

I believe the skills of which we develop in this life are carried through to the new life.

I believe by focusing on ourselves through developing high morals and strength of character develops our soul. This development of character and strength is carried with us in the next life making our future lives easier. We cannot take our material possessions with us, but we can take strength of character and skill developments with us.

If we develop psychic abilities, then we are more likely to carry these through to the next life. My father's wife believes she was a witch as she always had interests in casting spells and Wicca. However, she was always untrusting of others which makes sense if she was worried about being burnt at the stake in her past lives.

Those that seem to have it all, the looks, the money, should not be held in jealously for I believe that they have lived many lives and have developed great karma. They would have come back as various forms of different people and as such due to their evolved nature have been blessed with beauty and a good life. We should look up to these people rather than look to harm them.

Likewise, those that appear to have trouble

constantly were probably not good in a past life and are feeling that of which they inflicted. However, they need to rise above this karma to live a good life in their next life.

Finally, those that are popular, and everyone seems to like are probably people that have lived many lives and always had a positive connection with people that they have encountered, even if a short interaction.

Personally, I find when I am feeling low and I am struggling to move my career on or some other worldly problem, I am drawn back to spirituality to help me see the bigger picture in life.

Let's think about the bigger picture now. Why are we here? How did we get to be here? How did the world come together so beautifully?

We are made up of atoms: 6 Neutrons, 6 Protons, and 6 Electrons. They give us life. The nature of man, the beast 666. We have used atoms to create nuclear bombs. Bacteria, something so tiny, but yet can kill us. Insects can travel higher than us with their wings yet are constrained to the Earth's atmosphere, yet we can create vehicles to travel further than them.

Counties how you can be on one side of the planet freezing with ice, yet the other side of the planet hot and on dry desert. The Earth, the biosphere of life, 4.5 billion years old, how long have we lived on Earth?

The solar system, the sun takes up 99% of the mass of the solar system.

The milky way galaxy, our home galaxy, 10 to 100 billion solar systems are here.

Our local group cluster is made up of 54 galaxies.

The Virgo supercluster made up of 100 galaxy groups and clusters

The universe. At least 2 trillion galaxies are observable to the Hubble telescope.

All of that, can you imagine, then, throw on multi-universes.

WHY do we love? Why do we dream? Why do we have consciousness?

If, we simply, just die, then why do we remember things? Can we ever program a soul? Next time you go outside, and it is nighttime. Look up at the beauty of the universe, how long it took everything to make you. All the things that have led to making you in the universe. Look up tonight, to the sky!

119. Final Thoughts

Let me leave you on this note, if you do not think you can dream then think again as both human and animals dream, this has been proven by scientists.

Even a fruit fly has shown brain activity of being asleep (Galoustian, 2016). From simple to complex organisms, we all sleep (Zimmer, et al., 2015).

Reptiles have been found to share REM and slow-wave sleep patterns with mammals and birds (Shein-Idelson, et al., 2016), showing that sleep appeared in their early in evolution (Max-Planck-Gesellschaft, 2016).

Research (Schwab, et al., 2009) has shown babies dream with sleep cycles in the fetus starting after around seven months in the womb. The fetus spends most of its time sleep cycling every 20-40 minutes back and forth between REM and non-REM sleep.

References

Galoustian, G. (2016). *Sleep Tight, Fruit Fly - New Gene Identified.* Retrieved September 01, 2016, from www.fau.edu/newsdesk/articles/sleep-gene-study.php

Horikawa, T., Tamaki, M., Miyawaki, Y., & Kamitani, Y. (2013). Neural Decoding of Visual Imagery During Sleep. *Science, 340*(6132), 639-642.

Hudson, A. E., Calderon, D. P., Pfaff, D. W., & Proekt, A. (2014). Recovery of consciousness is mediated by a network of discrete metastable activity states. *PNAS, 111*(25), 9283-9288.

Irwin, K. (2014). *Study examines how brain 'reboots' itself to consciousness after anesthesia.* Retrieved September 01, 2016, from http://newsroom.ucla.edu/releases/study-examines-how-brain-reboots-itself-to-consciousness-after-anesthesia

Kamitani, Y., & Tong, F. (2005). Decoding the visual and subjective contents of the human brain. *Nature Neuroscience, 8,* 679-685.

Max-Planck-Gesellschaft. (2016). *Bearded dragons show REM and slow wave sleep.* Retrieved September 01, 2016, from https://www.mpg.de/10477322/reptiles-brain-sleep

Schwab, K., Groh, T., Schwab, M., & Witte, H. (2009). Nonlinear analysis and modeling of cortical activation and deactivation patterns in the immature fetal electrocorticogram. *Chaos: An Interdisciplinary Journal of Nonlinear Science, 19*(1), 015111. doi:https://doi.org/10.1063/1.3100546

Shein-Idelson, M., M. Ondracek, J., Liaw, H.-P., Reiter, S., & Laurent, G. (2016). Slow waves, sharp waves, ripples, and REM in sleeping dragons. *Science, 352*(6285), 590-595.

Stromberg, J. (2013). *Scientists Figure Out What You See While You're Dreaming.* Retrieved September 01, 2016, from https://www.smithsonianmag.com/science-nature/scientists-figure-out-what-you-see-while-youre-dreaming-15553304/

Zimmer, C., Wilson, M., Rattenborg, N., & Schenck, C. H. (2015). *The Mind After Midnight: Where Do You Go When You Go to Sleep?* Retrieved September 01, 2016, from https://www.worldsciencefestival.com/videos/the-mind-after-midnight-where-do-you-go-when-you-go-to-sleep/

ABOUT THE AUTHOR

Any experiences you have after reading this book please contact the author as they would love to hear about your experiences. The author can be contacted via:
email: s333phy@gmail.com

I wrote this book to give an insight, but I am not here to walk further into the spirt world with you. I am here to show you a path exists, but not here to guide you through it. I am here to discuss your experiences of the path after you have encountered it.

If you would like to share your experiences, please do as I absolutely love to hear other people's experiences. A movie director may create movies, but he does not limit himself to only his own movies.

There are some amazing people out there that are advanced in dreaming, lucid dreaming, out of body travel, energy work, shamanism, Reiki, and many other practices. Contact me and I can send you a list.

I suggest you **try many different people** as you can to gain awareness of all the different types of spiritual practices. Find what you resonate with and do not listen to others. Speak to those around you whom you feel will not judge you. You will be amazed at who in your family might have had interesting experiences, I found it was always the least expected family members.

If **you offer services** around any energy work, lucid dreaming, or other spiritual practices let me know and I can add your details to my list and forward your details to people if they ask me for further information.

Printed in Great Britain
by Amazon